WHAT IF?
THE ART OF
CRUSHING
ANXIETY

Erik W. Kieser

WHAT IF?

THE ART OF
CRUSHING
ANXIETY

The information in this book is designed to help you make informed choices about the treatment of anxiety and depression. This book is not intended as a substitute for professional medical advice, diagnosis, or treatment from a qualified health care provider. Anyone who is dealing with chronic anxiety and/or depression should seek the help of a professional in dealing with those conditions. You should always speak with your doctor or other qualified health care provider before you start, stop, or change any prescribed part of your care plan or treatment. Although the author and publisher have made every effort to ensure that the information was correct and accurate at the time of publication, the author and publisher do not assume and hereby disclaim any liability to any party for any loss, damage or disruption caused by errors or omissions, whether such errors or omissions result from negligence, accident or any other cause.

Book design, editing, production: Publishing Concierge, LLC
Editing: Rosalee Clarke
Cover design: Alexander Valchev
Printed in the United States of America
What If? The Art of Crushing Anxiety / Erik Kieser. —1st ed.
ISBN 978-0-9963652-6-0

Contents

Acknowledgments

It is the rare author who doesn't understand that no one writes a book alone. In the case of this book I owe many, many people for the knowledge, wisdom, compassion, care and support I've received, both during the years of my fight with anxiety and in the years that followed while I worked to develop the model and thinking presented in this book.

I must start with Dr. Jack Clarke, the therapist who first "pulled me from the water" as I was drowning in anxiety that terrible (and amazing) year of 1995. It is my (and many people's) great loss that Dr. Clarke passed away in 2017. His directness, skill and compassion were key in keeping me together long enough to find my way out of those dark, frightening days.

I'm also very much in debt to my partner of 18 years (and husband for the last two), Robert Clarke (no relation to Dr. Clarke, but an interesting coincidence, and, interestingly enough, also a therapist). He has been a tireless champion of my finishing this book, as well as the source of enormous encouragement, inspiration and patience while I labored to get this work done.

One of the most important figures in my life, and another inspiration and champion of this book, was my friend Laura Morefield. Friends for 30 years, Laura passed in the summer of 2011, and it was her diagnosis of colon cancer that pushed me to honor the promise I'd made to myself—a promise to write this book. My early conversations with her, her feedback on the blog that I wrote working on the content of this book, and her wry sense of humor were essential.

Still another champion of this work has been my sister, Kathryne Kieser. Kathryne has endured endless hours of phone conversations as I wrestled with language and explanation of concepts—thank you sister-mine! She has also helped me road-test much of the thinking in this book.

I owe a huge thanks to the good people of the Fear Mastery Facebook Group, and in specific Patty Cunningham, Donna Zeigler-Wood, Melissa Hayden, Lydia Gibas, Desiree Cherry and Lisa Stilts. The Facebook chats, the group discussions, the individual feedback and their efforts to apply this material all contributed mightily to this book's creation and final form.

Thanks goes also to Rosalee Clarke for her meticulous editing of this book in its final form. Her careful eye, brilliant sense of humor and passion for good grammar saved this writer from numerous technical errors. Any remaining mistakes are entirely my own!

Then there are the giants who have gone before this humble writer on the subject of anxiety. They include but are not limited to Dr. Susan Jeffers, Dr. Albert Ellis, Dr. Martin Seligman, Dr. Theodore Issac Rubin, Dr. M. Scott Peck, Dr. John Sarno, Dr. Andrew Weil, Robert M. Sapolsky, Melody Beattie and last, but most definitely not least, Ann Seagrave and Faison Covington in their work *Free From Fears*, the first material I ever found that spoke of dealing decisively with chronic anxiety. This book is very much an effort of standing on the shoulders of giants, and you can find all their works listed in my bibliography.

Finally, my thanks to Melody Marler, my editor, cheerleader and gifted manager of the editing and publishing process. While we live in the time of self-publishing, life would have been much more difficult without her expert guidance, patience and lovely sense of humor. Thank you Ms. Melody for partnering with me to get this work done—you helped make this dream into a reality.

Introduction

You're anxious. I'm guessing that because you're reading the beginning of this book. You might be experiencing or wrestling with anxiety in a variety of ways. You might be simply stressed at work, feeling too much pressure and wishing you had some techniques to turn off the chatter in your mind. You might be wrestling with some degree of chronic anxiety—a sense of a number of concerns that gnaw at your energy and time, but never escalate into anything as dramatic as panic attacks (acute anxiety).

Or you might be wrestling with panic attacks, and the fear of their coming on without warning. You might be only occasionally dealing with those debilitating experiences, or you might be under constant bombardment from them, living in terror of the next attack.

You could be in the grip of some level of depression, either occasional spells or long periods of what feels like the lights going out in your life. Or you might be wrestling with ALL of these various manifestations of anxiety.

You might be functioning pretty well in your life, and nobody even knows you're dealing with anxiety. You might be doing just OK, but dreading the feeling like the walls are beginning to close in. Or you might be lost in the worst-case situations that anxiety can produce—agoraphobia or being house-bound because you're afraid of just about everything, and/or fighting chronic, unrelieved depression.

Whatever your particular experience with anxiety, you want some relief; or, if you're shading into the more life-sucking side of anxiety, you want this crap to stop, and you want your life back.

You may have tried a variety of approaches to this problem. You could be using therapy or one or more medications prescribed by your doctor, in your efforts to get free. You may have experimented with meditation or exercise as ways to provide relief. You may have changed jobs, ended or started a relationship, relocated where you live, gone on a long trip or joined a self-help group.

It's possible you've received any one of a number of diagnoses: Generalized Anxiety Disorder, Illness Anxiety Disorder, Obsessive-Compulsive Disorder, just to name a few. You may have been told that your condition is only something that can, best case, be managed but never really dealt with and put behind you.

Or you may have kept all of your struggles and fears to yourself and done none of these things, not really being sure what the problem was or even having much faith that there was anything anyone could do. I'm further guessing that, whatever you have or haven't done to try and deal with your anxiety, you're feeling trapped to some extent, and you are worried that nobody really understands what you're dealing with at this point in your life. If you had Aladdin's magic lamp and could just make a wish, the first thing you'd do is ask the genie to relieve your anxiety, once and for all.

As I'll describe in this book, I've been in your shoes, for all of the above conditions. I am no stranger to chronic and acute anxiety. I first became aware of the extent and severity of my own anxiety in junior high school, even though I had no clue that it was anxiety I was dealing with, and sure as hell didn't know enough to do anything about it. I know how dark the days can get, how terrifying the nights can feel and how hopeless everything can come to seem.

I fought panic attacks and chronic anxiety for over twenty years, and that struggle included two close brushes with suicide. I eventually became agoraphobic, all but unable to go out into the world. I understand in a deeply personal way how fear can lock down and shut off a person's life, how fear can limit our belief in our range of options, even how fear can leave a person feeling as if there are no options at all.

During those years several people attempted to help me, with varying degrees of success. I am forever grateful to all of them, most of all to Dr. Jack Clarke and his use of the CHAANGE Program; he and it opened the door to hope for me. At the same time, it was very clear, even at the beginning of that work back in 1995, that the tools I had been offered were in a very real sense "first generation" tools. They were a good start, and with some work, proved useful in some circumstances.

What they didn't—and couldn't—do was give me a clean, lucid map of *why* I fought anxiety and fear the way I did. As a result, they couldn't explain consistently why something worked or didn't work, why the same tool or technique was sometimes effective and sometimes ineffective.

I was confronted with this again for a brief time in early 2003, when I dealt with obsessive-compulsive behavior as well as the leading edge of acute anxiety, something I had hoped I'd resolved years earlier. I had already fought free of panic attacks, and so to have even the shadow of another bout with serious anxiety made me (understandably) anxious! I sought out books and resources for help, and while some techniques and tools seemed to provide relief under some circumstances, sometimes I didn't find anything I could hang my hat on in the way of a clear, unified explanation of where my fear was coming from.

This was further complicated by the various diagnoses offered by the DSM-5, the book used by therapists and psychologists to assess various psychological and emotional conditions in their patients. There are no fewer than twelve different diagnosed conditions of anxiety in the current edition of the DSM, and they (at least in the way they are presented there) seem to describe different conditions that often need different approaches and tools.

At the same time, I can only describe my response to those descriptions as suspicious: why so many different ways to describe what sounded over and over again like simply different flavors of anxiety? My own experience and that of other people I'd talked to and read about, both with panic attacks and obsessive-compulsive behavior, seemed to indicate there were basics that linked all the different diagnoses of anxiety.

Having stated that, let me be very clear about what I am and what I'm not. I am not a therapist, a research psychologist, a doctor or a scientist. I am simply a guy who has wrestled with and almost been overcome by brutal, debilitating anxiety and depression for much of my life. For a very long time, I assumed that lack of professional expertise disqualified me to have any opinion or position on the nature and origins, let alone the treatment, of fear and anxiety. So when I noticed the similarities I just mentioned, I wasn't sure what to do with those observations.

Two things finally set me free to pursue the work of this book. The first was a promise I made to myself in 1995, the year I finally moved around the worst of the panic attacks. As I worked with, fumbled with and was often frustrated by the tools and techniques I had been offered in that year, I found myself thinking one afternoon that there had to be a clear, lucid map of fear and anxiety that explained those conditions across a wide range of experiences and symptoms. I couldn't explain why I was so sure that was true, but I knew it in my gut.

So I made a promise to myself that I was going to do my best to sort out, if I could, that map I was sure existed, a map of **why** we get anxious in the first place—the real origins of anxiety—and see if I could help assemble a better-organized toolbox of ways to get that anxiety managed more effectively.

The second was a slow-growing awareness that, in the years since the end of the full-on panic attacks, I had begun to see patterns in the way that fear and anxiety worked in my life. I became increasingly sure (from conversations, from reading, and from what other people did in response to their fear and anxiety) that those patterns might be very much like what other people experienced in their lives. This in turn strengthened my conviction that there was a basic map of anxiety that could be discovered and explained.

I began to work on what I've come to call the What If? Map—a single, clean, simple map of the origins and drivers of fear and anxiety. As a result of that map and the explanation it provides, I've found a clarity and a set of tools that have helped me put chronic anxiety and worry behind me in a decisive way.

Don't get me wrong: I still feel fear and anxiety. Of course I do. The elegant and highly useful mechanism that is the Flight or Fight response is with me (and all of us) always. As a result, I still react to fearful situations like drunk drivers or big snarling dogs with a burst of adrenaline, that workhorse of Flight or Fight. I still have my heart skip a beat when I watch a scary movie or see a bomb go off on TV.

What I will not now do, however, is make a habit of treating problems as crises—the real reason we get and keep anxiety in our lives. As a result, I avoid the quicksand of chronic fear and anxiety. I understand the reasons I start getting lost in worry, anxiety and fear, and I know what to do to shut it down.

My goal with this book is to clarify this understanding

for anyone who is tired of feeling frightened and

trapped a significant amount—or all—of the time.

That group includes people who fight panic attacks, chronic or ongoing anxiety that never quite progresses to panic attacks, and those of us who have gotten mired in a repetitive cycle of depression. (I believe depression usually stems directly from long-term anxiety, whether we are conscious of that anxiety or not.)

Some people reading this may tell themselves, "Well, this is nice—a book for people who deal with chronic anxiety and fear. Good for them! I, however, don't have any real fears—I'm pretty grounded/happy/fearless." I hope that's true for you. Then again, you did pick up this book, so it's entirely likely that this book could be useful to you as well. Read the following questions and see if any of these concerns apply to you:

- Do you carry ongoing worries about your job, your finances or your career?
- Are you constantly anxious about your retirement?

- Does watching the news leave you angry, depressed, frightened or just blue?
- Do you sometimes feel like you're not in control of your thinking, your feelings or where your life is headed?
- Do you wish you could do or live part or all of your life differently, but also feel helpless or stuck in your present way of living?

If you answered yes to any of these questions, then this book has some useful information and tools to offer you. It's entirely possible that you've locked away, out there past the walls of your Comfort Zone, fears and worries to which you no longer give much conscious thought. And consciously or not, you have little interest in bringing those worries and anxieties back to active consideration. That makes a great deal of sense, because to do so risks rocking the boat and introducing increased worry and concern in your life.

Please don't misunderstand me. I'm not interested

in conjuring fears where there are none in your life.

There's plenty of fear and worry to go around without

generating more.

But I assume you picked up this book for a reason. The goal of this book is to explain why we learn to fear what we fear, as well as give you a set of tools to master those fears, whether you're in the grip of chronic anxiety and depression, or whether you realize there are serious concerns or worries you'd like to address but find the whole idea unnerving. This map isn't hard to learn, and the tools are not complicated either; you'll grasp them quickly and, with practice, you'll find you can apply them with increasing skill.

Wherever you find yourself in the work of addressing your worries and fears, the challenge will come in two ways: 1) deciding to actually take on your fear(s), and 2) giving yourself some time and effort to get skillful with the tools to do so.

In my chase, I longed for a pill or a two-step, half-hour technique that would end my fear and worry quickly, painlessly and without lots of struggle, and certainly no more fear. And as I'm sure you know, tens of millions of people in the U.S. alone are using anti-anxiety and anti-depression medication on a daily basis; you may be one of them. There are tens of millions more that medicate with alcohol, a variety of legal and illegal drugs, food, gambling and an amazing collection of other ways to keep the fear at bay. All of us who wrestle with ongoing fear and worry want nothing more than a relief from that fear. And we want it NOW.

But medication can't end anxiety at its source; it can't bring permanent relief, because the source of fear and anxiety lies in our thinking, and the feelings/physical sensations that are the responses to that thinking. And the only real road to easing and ending that fear and anxiety is to address and change that thinking.

....

Sound simple? It is. But simple isn't the same as

instant, and it takes some deliberate, sustained work,

which means it will take some time.

....

There's nothing in these statements about dealing with fear and anxiety that's original to me. The psychologist Albert Ellis started this conversation decades ago in books such as *The Power of Rational Thinking* and *Feeling Better, Getting Better, Staying Better*, explaining that thoughts cause feelings, and thoughts can override and change those feelings.

But despite this excellent, powerful thinking and writing about fear, most of us still live in prisons of our own making, unsure what to do about it, often terrified to give it too much thought, and all but convinced we're doomed to failure if we try anyway. We feel this way because we are in the grip of a reflex (Flight or Fight) that evolved hundreds of millions of years ago. While it is just about perfect for the conditions it evolved for, in the presence of our thinking and worry it essentially malfunctions, leaving us reactive, afraid, and in retreat from what frightens us.

We must first 1) understand that we are creating our anxiety in our thinking (even though in the beginning we are not doing this consciously or deliberately), and 2) face down that mechanism called Flight or Fight, understand what's really going on in our bodies and emotions, and learn to manage it in the ways that will set us loose from and provide mastery over that fear.

Please, don't simply take my word for any of this. Read the book, test the model and try the tools. It would be outstanding if I could promise you instant relief. I would have loved such a promise myself during the years I suffered from increasing anxiety, fear, panic attacks, and finally agoraphobia and depression.

But what I can promise you is, regardless of how you may feel at this moment, you are smarter, stronger and tougher than your fears. You don't have to stay a prisoner of your fears. You can master your fear, and you don't have to consume years of your life to do so.

There may be no more powerful experience in our personal lives than when we break past a fear or anxiety we've carried for years. The sense of freedom, the awareness of personal power, and the expanded universe we move into when we conquer a fear are amazing. Who doesn't want to shake free of their limiting anxiety and fear?

That we can't instantly master our anxiety can be hard to hear—even scary—when we're feeling trapped and helpless by what worries us. It will mean challenging some long-held assumptions in our thinking, including what feelings mean, and what we should do about those feelings.

It will mean challenging your Comfort Zone, that learned set of boundaries and fears, and this can also feel frightening. It will require some questioning of your habit of living in and anticipating your future, and instead working to create a life centered on living in the present moment. But the payoff is nothing less than your freedom, real freedom, from chronic anxiety and fear. This is work that can be done, and you can do it.

You'll probably find this book most useful if you treat it as a workbook and a toolbox. Write in it, argue with it, throw it across the room, engage with it. Like any toolbox, you'll only find it useful if you take what's in it and try it out. Remember that learning new skills and new ways of thinking takes effort and time; be patient with yourself and the process. Anxiety isn't a mystery. The tools to break the hold of anxiety are not complicated. It will take work, time and a willingness to challenge some of the assumptions you hold about your life and the world—but it is work anyone can do.

You'll encounter a host of feelings, and some of those won't be very comfortable. That's OK—you're already uncomfortable with your anxiety and fear, or you wouldn't be looking at this book. In the words of Peter McWilliams, start to get your head around the notion that we each need to gain some comfort with being uncomfortable in this work. It means you're tackling your fears and making headway against them.

So, are you ready to start shaking free of anxiety and fear? Are you ready to stop letting fear dictate your thinking and your behavior, and instead turn the Flight or Fight response back to what it originally developed to do, which is keep you safe from immediate physical danger? It's my suspicion that you've given enough lifespan, energy, blood and treasure away to your fears. You don't have to give away any more.

CHAPTER 1

"What If?" Thinking

"What" and "if"—two words as nonthreatening as words come. But put them together, side-by-side, and they have the power to haunt you for the rest of your life: What if?

Letters to Juliet

S ince the beginning of our species, fear has been one of the most vital tools available to human development. In fact, it can be said that fear is essential to survival.

Creatures without fear will sooner or later be caught in one of the various dangers and perils that make up the natural world, and they will, in all likelihood, not survive. We human beings have a healthy capacity to react with fear in the face of danger.

Yet our modern world appears awash in fear and anxiety. Most news reports seem tailored to create a fearful or worried response, as the media bombards us with stories of plane crashes, oil leaks, financial disasters, dark predictions of social or political upheaval, and all with constant warnings that things are about to fall apart. We worry about our income, our health, our family, our job, our country, and our world. We even worry that we worry too much!

The challenge in the work to understand anxiety starts with getting some clarity around just what danger actually IS, versus what generates anxious thinking, and then from that understanding to become much better managers of the natural anxiety response we have that helps us survive. **We have to get clear when we actually are in danger, as opposed to when we think we're in danger.**

This becomes even more important in the face of the ongoing evidence that one of the things we should actually be a little concerned with is how much energy and focus we give to being anxious and fearful so much of the time. Robert Sapolsky discusses this in great and articulate detail in *Why Zebras Don't Get Ulcers.*

An enormous amount of stress comes from constant worry and anxiety stemming from our fears of what might happen, what could be if our fears are realized—i.e., we believe we are in danger, and so we are reacting mentally and physically as if we are actually at risk for our lives.

This is precisely what this book is about—how thinking is the source of the vast majority of anxiety, and how we need to change our thinking to get free of anxiety as a constant companion.

For that discussion to make sense we have to get clear about the actual origins of our anxiety—"what if?" thinking and the Flight or Fight response. And to do that effectively we first have to be clear on two kinds of thinking we humans do: problem thinking and crisis thinking.

PROBLEM VS. CRISIS THINKING

Any time we face a situation we have the potential to bring one of two kinds of thinking to bear on that situation. We can either treat the situation, whatever it is, as a problem, or we can respond to it as if it were a crisis. This is the exact pivot point from which anxiety either starts or fails to start.

And when I say anything, I mean anything—any challenge, issue, ongoing dilemma, or even no apparent issue at all, just a situation or context in which we live. The issue isn't really ever the thing—it is how we think about it, how we react to it, that drives whether we will generate anxiety about it or not.

So what does it mean to approach something by treating it as a problem? In this discussion of anxiety, it is actually easier to discuss what happens when we DON'T treat a situation as a problem, but instead react to it as a crisis.

Crisis thinking is simply this: we think/believe that we are at immediate risk for injury or death, and if we don't do something right now we will be injured or even killed. I'm certain every person reading this book has some experience in their lives where they can instantly say, "Oh, yeah, I know what that's like!"

It could be that drunk driver that started swerving right in front of you on the freeway years ago. Before you were even conscious of responding you were taking action to get clear of that maniac, to get out of his or her way. Maybe it was the time you saw your child fall from a tree they were climbing, or heard them shout or scream from their bedroom. You were flying up the stairs or into the backyard before you were even aware that you were reacting.

When that happened, you were in the grip of what I mentioned earlier—the Flight or Fight response. You decided, at light speed, that there was an immediate crisis, and your highly evolved and ancient Flight or Fight response took over and started making things happen to get you or your loved ones to safety.

I'll talk more about crisis thinking and reacting when I discuss the Flight or Fight response in greater detail (and there's a lot to say about Flight or Fight and its relation to anxious thinking.) The bottom line for this part of the discussion is that crisis thinking is strongly reactive thinking—it has to be. If you're actually in a crisis there isn't a lot of time to ponder what to do. You have to take action NOW or you're at risk of something terrible happening! It's really remarkable what thinking we *can* do when we're in crisis, but it is still very much crisis thinking. But now let's compare crisis thinking to problem thinking.

I could almost define problem thinking as not crisis thinking—i.e., that when we are treating a situation as a problem we are not treating that situation as an immediate risk for injury or death. Problem thinking is not reactive thinking, which is exactly what crisis thinking has to be. Problem thinking assumes that whatever is in front of us will take a little time and thought. It assumes that there may have to be some information gathered, some options considered, even some experiments run on the situation, before resolution is reached/a solution is found.

When somebody says, "What's for dinner?" we begin to do problem thinking (well, we do if we are not treating the question as a crisis). We ponder what's in the fridge, we consider going out to eat, we discuss what people want for dinner, etc. We treat the issue of dinner as a problem, and eventually we come up with a solution, or at least attempt a solution.

....

We can't escalate to anxiety if we're treating an issue

as a problem. Period.

....

That's worth saying again: we can't escalate to anxiety if we treat an issue as a problem. But we can and do escalate to anxiety if we engage in crisis thinking. This is huge, this simple notion. **It is the source of the vast majority of anxious thinking.**

To be anxious (and to treat as a crisis) something that IS a crisis is brilliant, a great survival tool. To be anxious (and to treat as a crisis) something that isn't a crisis—really anything that won't kill or wound you seriously in the next five minutes—that's the origin of long-term, debilitating anxiety.

....

The challenge for those of us who fight anxiety is that
we have learned to deal with a giant array of issues as
crises when they are really simply problems.

....

I will discuss and give examples of that array a little later on,
but for the moment we need to understand how we get to crisis
thinking in the first place—by starting "what if?" thinking that
in turn fires up Flight or Fight.

"WHAT IF?" THINKING AND THE FLIGHT OR FIGHT RESPONSE

To understand anxiety is to understand one central idea: the
vast majority of anxiety starts in our thinking. There are a host
of physical and emotional responses to anxious thinking, and we
often confuse those responses as being the cause of our anxiety,
but the fact remains that anxiety is a thinking problem.

That last paragraph may sound wrong to you—or at the least,
counter-intuitive. Anxiety seems to be much more about how
we feel, emotionally and physically, than anything to do with
our thinking. Many anxiety fighters report that they can't really
identify any specific things they are thinking about or are afraid
of in the moment. I understand that answer, and will explain this
more fully a little later.

Those powerful feelings, those strong sensations we experience
when we are anxious, are the reactions of the Flight or Fight response. (This is traditionally called the Fight or Flight response,
but I've reversed the words for a reason I'll explain a little later on.) There's no question that Flight or Fight, the mechanism

humans have to react to real, physical, immediate danger, is responding to our anxiety—but it all begins with thinking. A large part of the confusion about which comes first, anxious thinking or anxious physical and emotional reactions, comes from how the brain works. Let's discuss that for a minute.

THE FOUNDATIONAL ABILITIES THAT MAKE "WHAT IF?" THINKING GO

How does it start? To answer that question, we have to talk a little bit about the brain. Human brains are amazing. They have extraordinary powers, powers that can be used to do a host of useful things—solve complex problems, create art, coordinate large groups of people, conceive of things that are brand new, and much more.

But they are also capable of taking those powers and making us very, very anxious. There are several things our amazing brains do that contribute to anxious thinking. The first is how the human brain makes decisions about what is and isn't safe. Peter McWilliams and others have termed that learned framework of safety the Comfort Zone.

This is often classically described as the zebra going down to the watering hole to get a drink, only to be attacked by a hungry lion. The zebra, getting away from the crazy creature that wants to eat it, is way more wary the next time he or she hits the watering hole—they have learned potential danger is there.

This applies to humans as well. We learn where the "lions" are in our lives, real and assumed, and then start to avoid them. Notice the use of the word "assumed" in that last sentence. This is how we create our Comfort Zones. Way, way too often, those

Comfort Zones are full of things we're treating as crises, when what we're really dealing with are problems.

That wariness is transmitted through the body and emotions. The zebra, not having the amazing brains you and I do, doesn't consciously think to itself, "Gee, I'd better be careful around that watering hole—I've run into lions there before." It feels the warning of its Comfort Zone, and that warning is part of the mechanism of Flight or Fight.

The problem of anxious thinking in humans is that it doesn't start with actual danger, like the zebra and the lion. All it takes for us is to think, estimate, and anticipate danger in the future (five minutes from now, two years from now, ten years from now), and anxious thinking can begin to take hold.

The brain constructs a story of the world as it moves through the world. You might almost say that the brain is creating a movie about what's happening to you, minute by minute. That story helps you make sense of the world, organize things in your life and explain how things seem to work.

Notice the word "seems" there. Just because the brain thinks it understands how something is or should be or is supposed to work doesn't necessarily mean it's right—just that it has settled on an explanation. Keep that in mind in this discussion of the brain.

So the brain creates a map of the world around us. We then tend to rely on that map as basically accurate. This mapmaking is very useful to us, as it creates the assumptions we make about the world and how it works. Chairs tend to hold us, pizza tends to taste yummy, babies are almost invariably cute (unless they need their diaper changed). The brain tends to assume that we have a working map of the world.

When it works, this mapmaking is great. But it can also lead us to make assumptions that are NOT true, not useful, or even directly harmful to us. You could say that we're only as good as our maps. If your map has errors, then you're going to take wrong directions.

Another remarkable capacity of the human brain is its ability to automate large amounts of our daily behavior. We call those automated programs "habits." Think of brushing your teeth or folding your laundry. You are rarely conscious of what you're doing when you're doing those habitual routines.

This is an incredible ability, since your brain is then free to do lots of other things—ponder why France is so far away, plan for world domination—whatever actually requires your brain to think consciously. This is important to understand when we discuss anxiety because we don't always have habits that are as innocuous as tooth-brushing. Sometimes we develop less-than-useful habits—anxious thinking habits—and they can really take our thinking sideways.

You might say the stories/map we create to understand our world then get automated into habits. Once we think we've "drawn the map," we turn it over to our automatic, habitual thinking.

....

Then off we go, merrily (or anxiously) moving through

our world, not really conscious of a great deal of our

thinking, but simply responding in a habitual way TO

our world as we go.

....

There is one more item to add to our list of amazing brain qualities: Humans also have an ability to conjecture about the future. We can estimate things that might happen, think about them, even make decisions about them and plans to deal with them, despite the fact that they haven't happened and are not yet real. That ability makes planning possible. It also helps us avoid potential risk. We can anticipate and even get out of the way of problems or issues that could make trouble for us with this very human capacity. Nice ability, yes?

We can, however, also get lost in that future thinking—and turn it into anxious worrying about the future. This is the source of that "what if?" thinking I mentioned earlier. Humans ask a lot of "what if?" questions. Not all of them are anxious, but a great number of them are, and these questions form the foundation of anxious thinking.

As we get lost in anticipating, we can start treating our thinking about the future as if it were already real—as if it was happening to us right now.

Ugh. Not so useful. In fact, we can seriously derail ourselves by working to anticipate, analyze and react to the future as if our "what if?" thinking were the truth about that future.

So let's summarize these brain qualities discussed so far:

- The brain, as it moves through the world, decides what is safe and what isn't, and then sets up tripwires to warn us we are close to things that we have labeled as dangerous. This is called the Comfort Zone.

- The brain builds a map of the world and makes sense of the world through that map, including where the boundaries of safety (our Comfort Zone) are.
- The brain automates behavior it does over and over again, chunking it into dozens and hundreds of little programs we call habits.
- The brain has the ability to anticipate and plan for the future—and it will respond to that anticipating as if it was already real—i.e., engage in "what if?" thinking.

So why do we care about these abilities in relation to anxiety? Because these are the foundation stones upon which we build anxiety.

THE START OF "WHAT IF?" THINKING
AND THE ANXIETY IT CAN CREATE

"What if?" thinking can begin around just about any subject or issue that concerns us. It starts with the seed of a belief, an assumption, a personal standard that tells us how things should be, how we must be, what we can and can't do, how we should behave, etc.

This thinking springs directly from the map of the world that we create for ourselves. Of course, when I say "we create," I'm also including all the thinking that was handed to us by the people who helped us create our maps: our parents, our siblings, our teachers, our friends, our co-workers and bosses, etc.

And let's NOT underestimate the contribution our learning from other people contributes to the life-suck that is anxious thinking and reacting. The seeds of belief/assumption/personal standards mentioned above start to a large extent with what other people in our lives have tossed at us over the years of our lives, especially early on. They didn't necessarily set out to give us those anxious thought beginnings, but give them they did, and we made them our own.

I suspect this sounds very abstract. Let me give a concrete example of "what if?" thinking. I'll start with one of the most common fears in the world—the fear of speaking to an audience. I have spent a lot of time in my professional life teaching people to do presentations. At first I assumed the work would be mostly about the technical aspects of speaking—how to create an outline, how to set up visual aids, how to stay focused on the points the presenter needed to make, etc.

But it became clear pretty quickly that for most people the technical issues were secondary to their real and immediate need to be less afraid of speaking to a group. When I began exploring the fears of my students I began to hear common themes:

What if people laugh at me/make fun of my efforts to speak?

What if I make a mistake?

What if I look like I'm stupid?

What if people think I'm ugly/unattractive?

What if I freeze in front of the audience and can't talk?

What if I freak out/have a panic attack at the front of the room?

The majority of students were simply anxious about getting up and speaking. Most students in my classes made progress only when they, to some extent, dealt with their fears and overcame them.

Let's just take one fear here—the fear of people laughing at or making fun of a speaker—and map it onto the way "what if?" fears get started. Somewhere along the way, a student develops a sense that people laughing at or making fun of them is DANGEROUS. Maybe it was from things their parents or siblings or friends at elementary school (or even earlier) said. Maybe they tried something brave or new and someone made fun of them, and their takeaway from the experience was that being made fun of was terrible, risky, and something to be avoided.

Compare this with the kid who learns that doing something wacky, silly or brave is rewarding—it gets them attention, and brings them praise or positive feedback. Did you know any kids like that growing up? Clearly we can learn different lessons from each other and from our life experiences.

The bottom line is the first kid learned that drawing laughter or ridicule was a risky thing to do. In their thinking they drew a Comfort Zone boundary around that risk, warning them to stay away from situations where such risks might exist.

This boundary got included into the map of the world they were building. It became "truth" to them— something they assumed was fact.

And in assuming that, they developed a habit of thinking and in turn reacting cautiously any time these situations presented themselves.

Invited to speak at a friend's wedding, they shake their heads nervously and say, "No thanks," explaining how they really don't feel comfortable doing that, or they would embarrass their hosts by speaking. Told at work they need to present to clients to advance their career, they become very anxious and look for ways to avoid such presentations at all costs, even putting their jobs at risk in a desperate effort to stay away from their fear.

Because they are anticipating the danger of being made fun of and have created the habit of automatically thinking and reacting about what MIGHT happen, they're generating "what if?" thinking. That scares them, just as much as if they were actually in front of the group speaking and someone started to laugh at them. Presto—they're anxious. They may not even be aware of their fear, at least not consciously; they just feel this is a bad idea, and they are already in motion, reacting to that fear, backing away from it.

This is "what if?" thinking. Dr. Albert Ellis called this "should" thinking in his book *Feeling Better, Getting Better, Staying Better.* We develop a vast list of shoulds and shouldn'ts, musts and mustn'ts, cans and can'ts—and we rarely know we've assembled the lists we've created. This is just one more way to describe the "what if?" thinking we're working hard to avoid in our thinking and in our lives.

THE TENDENCY OF "WHAT IF?" THINKING, LEFT UNATTENDED, TO GROW AND SPREAD

One of the hardest things to understand is how much we are unaware of our "what if?" thinking. It's there in the back of our brains, lurking, and left to itself it has a bad way of growing, slowly, over time, and reaching into other aspects/concerns in our thinking.

Part of that comes from the feelings anxious thinking generates—that Flight or Fight response that evolved to keep us safe. We are largely (or even completely) unaware we're flinching back from our anxious feelings/reactions, but that's exactly what we're doing. In our flinching back, the feelings/sensations ease, and we feel better, at least for a long while. And this begins a nasty habit of retreating from our fearful thinking and reacting. Without a conscious awareness of the pattern, we begin retreating from anything that makes us uncomfortable or anxious.

So to continue my example of a fear of speaking to an audience, we might find ourselves growing uncomfortable with ANY situation where we might look foolish, make a mistake, or have people ridicule us. It's amazing how many people flee from just this one example of fearful thinking.

We don't really think about what we're doing. We're not aware we're slowly retreating from this or that aspect of living.

But we are in retreat, and slowly, over time, our Comfort Zones, those tripwires of personal safety we're always creating, push us back toward what feels like safety, away from the situations, issues or problems we've started treating like crises.

To understand this retreating more clearly, it's useful to understand the specifics of this Flight or Fight response. This powerful human ability has enormous influence over us if we're not clear on why it fires up and why we feel the way it makes us feel.

CHAPTER 2

Flight or Fight: An Explanation

Everything you want is on the other side of fear.
Jack Canfield

As I outlined in Chapter 1, we are the owners of a remarkable, powerful and highly automatic system called Flight or Fight.

The moment we think we're in danger this workhorse of safety powers up, and it has one mission: to get us away from whatever danger we think we're about to experience.

Notice in that first paragraph I said, "Whatever danger we *think* we're about to experience." We have to believe/think that we're in danger before Flight or Fight activates in our brains and bodies. How does that activation start physically, and how does it drive our anxiety?

One of our most remarkable abilities is the response to danger, a system commonly called Fight or Flight.

....

As I mentioned in Chapter 1, I have reversed this to

Flight or Fight because we are compelled first to run,

and only fight when we have to.

....

This mechanism for getting us to safety is fueled by two things: 1) our thinking (telling ourselves we're in danger) and 2) a chemical reaction powered by adrenaline and other hormones in our body. When we are faced with danger, real or perceived, our brain fires up Flight or Fight, and an impressive host of physical, emotional, and mental responses follows.

It makes for interesting reading, seeing just how fast this process takes place. In the natural world we rarely have a lot of time to gear up when we're faced with real, actual, physical danger. We have to get ready, in the real world, faced with real danger, NOW.

There is a lot to this getting-ready process. I'll describe that in a bit , but it's important to understand at this point that the body and brain do a host of things to deal with danger, and getting ready is at the heart of all the physical, emotional and mental reactions we experience when we're in the midst of anxiety.

The primary mission of Flight or Fight is to get us away from danger. Running is our first, best strategy. Why run first? Running is a great, even the most optimal, survival strategy. When a creature runs from danger and gets away, it gets to live and run another day. Just as importantly, it does so uninjured—i.e., in the best shape possible to continue living. This is engraved down in our very genes, this tendency to want to flee in the face of sudden danger. You can see this tendency even in the large predators—lions, tigers, wolves. When surprised or startled their first instinct is to flinch, step back, and even run away.

The "Fight" part of Flight or Fight is, in the natural world, what we do only when we can't run. We turn and fight when there is no way, at the moment, to get away from the danger we are facing in the here and now.

Fighting is risky. Fighting means we might get injured. Fighting means that, even if we win the fight, we might not be in the best position to carry on in the world. From a natural world perspective, it puts us at risk for producing and caring for offspring—and there is no higher priority in the natural world than that.

So we tend to fight only until we see an avenue of escape. That escape might be winning the fight—dealing with the danger decisively—or it might be running away.

This has huge implications for anyone who fights anxiety. I'll talk more about this after we review the various ways our bodies and brains get ready to deal with danger—when Flight or Fight fires up.

OUR BODY'S PHYSICAL RESPONSES

So let's say that you are faced with a real-world, actual dangerous situation. Let's go back to that drunk driver I mentioned in Chapter 1. There you are, minding your own business, thoughts far away from the routine of driving, when suddenly the car in front of you starts to swerve, weave or act erratically. Let's say they are right in front of you, and you're suddenly hyper-aware that this driver is putting your safety at risk.

In other words, you shout "DANGER!" to your brain, and your brain takes action, firing up Flight or Fight. In your body, a cluster of things happens in seconds.

The body starts to shut down blood flow to the "unnecessary" body parts for the duration of the crisis (i.e., the parts we won't need to run or fight right now, like our stomachs or our sex organs or our immune system).

This explains the nausea in our stomachs when we're anxious—digestion slows or even stops, because digesting food takes energy we divert to running and dealing with danger. This also explains the dry mouth many of us experience when we're in the grip of anxiety—saliva is part of digestion and it also slows down or even stops.

Flight or Fight also restricts blood flow to places that are more likely to get bitten or cut in our efforts to run or fight, like our fingers and toes—those parts of us that are flapping out there away from the center of our body. Remember, the whole mission is to get clear of the danger and live another day—and that works better if we don't lose a lot of blood in injuries.

Our heartbeat goes up, often way up, as we start pumping the body full of oxygen to get ready for that sprint we're about to make. Respiration goes up to match that need for oxygen, and so we're breathing faster and more shallowly.

We usually start to sweat too—all that energy coursing through our body heats things up, and we need to start dumping that heat, which is what sweating does. We also become more sensitive to stimuli around us—our hearing and vision and even our sense of smell can improve/sharpen, as we get very alert for what's happening around us during this moment of danger.

Impressive, yes? For a complete list of the physical reactions to Flight or Fight see Chapter 9.

Why tell you all this? I'm doing this because it is crucial, in our work to deal with anxiety and fear, that we understand that there is nothing weird or strange about any of these physical responses. They all make perfect sense in light of what is happening during the experience of Flight or Fight.

....

What makes them scary is that they are very strong,

seem to come out of nowhere, and they seem to be

telling us to get the hell away from whatever we're

labeling as dangerous/scary.

....

That also makes sense. There isn't time, in the presence of real danger, to do a lot of pondering or contemplating about the situation. We need to get moving. This also explains so much of those emotions we experience when we are in the midst of Flight or Fight.

OUR FEELINGS/EMOTIONAL RESPONSES

Our emotions also get fired up by Flight or Fight, with the goal of getting us moving during this drunk driver moment we're experiencing. Science is still coming to understand exactly how all that works in the brain—it is an impressively complex set of activities. The bottom line here is simply the need to get moving. And what could be better than getting us emotionally fired up and energized so we will definitely take action?

In a sense, we're scaring the crap out of ourselves to get moving. When you have that surge of worry/fear/anxiety/terror flood through your body, you either get moving or you freeze in place, which is another way of running from the danger, with the idea that if they can't see us they can't hurt us.

Same thing for anger/rage/upset—these get us ready to fight! These emotions supply us with motivation and energy, and so we're ready to deal with whatever we need to do in that moment—make like the wind, or find a handy tree branch and get ready to fight this danger to a standstill.

In the example of the drunk driver, we might suddenly slam on the brakes in an effort to get away from the lunatic in front of us. Or if we can't just get out of the way—swerve, stop, etc.—we will experience rage, anger, or fury at this person putting us at risk. That fury and anger can fuel serious action on our parts, all in an effort to deal with this real-world crisis.

The rush of fearful and anxious and angry feelings is gearing us up to deal with whatever needs to happen in that moment. There's nothing mysterious about that rush of feelings—it is a completely natural, normal response to danger.

There are other shades of feeling/emotion that surface during a bout with Flight or Fight. We can feel embarrassed, guilty, sad, or a host of other emotions in the turbulence of our frightened thinking. None of them are odd, none of them mean anything except that we are in the grip of Flight or Fight.

Most of us won't be particularly troubled when we experience these various emotions during an actual crisis. We expect to be deeply moved or even shaken up when we're dealing with real danger. Things get weird, however, when we're dealing with anxiety, because either it's not obvious why we're having a torrent of emotions (and unexplained physical reactions) or because we can't seem to control those feelings. (For a complete list of the emotional reactions to Flight or Fight see Chapter 9.)

And the fun doesn't stop there. While our emotions and physical reactions are in turmoil we are also experiencing psychological reactions to Flight or Fight.

OUR THINKING/PSYCHOLOGICAL RESPONSES

Thinking is impacted by the rush of Flight or Fight. Some of us believe we can't think at all when we're anxious, but that's not true. We can't think in the same way we can think when we're not anxious, but we definitely have access to our thinking.

What does happen to thinking during this rush is that it narrows, focuses, and limits its efforts in order to best serve Flight or Fight—i.e., to either help us get away or help us do the best we can in defending ourselves. So, for example, our higher-order, abstract thinking abilities become limited, or can all but shut down entirely when we are in the midst of a crisis. Contemplating the nature of reality, or what color works best for the paint in the bathroom, doesn't matter when you're dealing with a drunk driver in your way.

....

Instead, your thinking is focused very narrowly on one thing: how in the hell are you going to not get into an accident with this person? In these moments, you are looking for clear routes of escape, and your brain is working very, very quickly. Thinking can take on a diamond-like clarity—but only in this narrow band.

....

On the other hand, if you can't see your way clear, thinking can get muddy, even panicky, and then you'll be at that point of preparing to fight, somehow, to get through the situation.

Other things happen to us mentally in this context. One is that we find ourselves summoning up past experience when we were in danger—what did we do then? This is happening very fast— we need that information now.

We also can have a sense of being completely or partly detached from what is happening—this is sometimes called dissociation. This is a remarkable aspect of the psychological response to anxiety. We get a sense of distance, detachment, almost the sense of being outside of time or reality. (This is why it sometimes feels like things are suddenly moving slowly in the midst of a traumatic event like a car accident or the example of encountering a drunk driver.)

This can be exceptionally helpful as we deal with a real crisis, but can be very disconcerting or even terrifying to someone who isn't in crisis, but is battling anxiety. This is a recurring problem with all the responses of Flight or Fight—they don't necessarily rock our worlds when they are happening in the clear context of a real emergency, but just about any of them can seem weird, frightening, or terrifying when they happen during our experience with anxiety.

We can also experience a sense of disorientation, or even become unclear where we are or what we were doing in the face of extreme anxiety. Stuttering is still another psychological response to Flight or Fight. This is again a symptom of non-essential functions (in this case, coherent communication) suffering from Flight or Fight's primary focus on getting us to safety.

Again, there is nothing weird or mysterious in this rush of experiences during Flight or Fight. They are all part of what happens, and are to be expected to a greater or lesser degree.

REAL DANGER VS. PERCEIVED DANGER, AND THE HARDWIRED NATURE OF FLIGHT OR FIGHT

To understand clearly Flight or Fight and its relation to anxiety, we have to be clear on two things: Flight or Fight (really, our automatic defense system might be a better name for it) can't tell between real danger or perceived danger. If we tell ourselves we're in danger, then Flight or Fight is going to activate. Period.

The other thing to understand about Flight or Fight is that it is, quite literally, hard-wired into our brains and bodies. This is a very old part of being human—indeed, of being a living creature on Earth. The moment Flight or Fight is activated in us, it isn't going to be shut down or stopped by force of will. **It will only stop when we think we're out of danger.**

None of this is a problem when we're actually in danger! Flight or Fight developed in living creatures to deal with real danger. When there was no real danger present, it didn't activate. Think for a moment about a gazelle on the plains of Africa, making its way through its gazelle day. Life consists of grazing, bringing up baby, and finding the next waterhole. Flight or Fight stays quiet until the moment that gazelle catches the scent of lion—otherwise gazelle life is pretty much worry-free.

Why worry-free? Because a gazelle isn't worrying about tomorrow or even five minutes from now. Just like us it has a first-rate emergency response system hard-wired into its brain and body, and it will deal with danger when it shows up.

THE PROBLEM ISN'T PHYSICAL DANGER

If we humans only had to deal just with the risks of living in the physical world we'd be as calm as those gazelles, at least most of the time. But we are not gazelles. We human beings have a second level of concerns to manage, unlike the rest of the creatures in the natural world. We have the blessings and challenges of intelligence to manage as well, and that's where anxiety and fear can become a problem.

This is a problem for a very simple reason: some of the concerns and problems we face in our lives can frighten us. **Not all of them—even those of us who have been mired in panic attacks and deep depression still have issues that don't rock our worlds—but some of them can and do.** When we begin to do "what if?" thinking—if we start making potential or real problems into crises, emergencies, in our thinking—then we run the risk of activating Flight or Fight.

....

The bottom line here is this: we have one system (Flight or Fight) to deal with physical danger, but we have two sources of fear. Our miraculous system to deal with real, physical danger doesn't recognize the difference between real, physical danger and danger in our thinking; it treats them exactly the same when activated by our thinking.

....

And once we've activated Flight or Fight with anxious thinking it is going to run its course. Worse, it's going to fire up just about any time we engage that anxious thinking, and it's going to keep firing up until we either stop making a crisis of whatever we're thinking about in the first place or we, however briefly, stop thinking about it.

In people who are dealing with anxiety on a regular basis, this can develop into what might be called a second layer of fears, on top of the fears that fire up Flight or Fight in the first place. We can teach ourselves, unwittingly, to be afraid of Flight or Fight sensations, emotions or psychological responses as well as the original "what if?" thinking that started the ball rolling in the first place.

Actually, this happens to most people around one or more fears, but it becomes particularly noxious when we find ourselves sliding into ongoing, escalating anxiety battles—chronic anxiety, panic attacks, etc. Most of us develop fears around specific elements of the responses of Flight or Fight; we focus on one or more symptoms and then treat those as crises as well.

We do that because we're operating largely in ignorance of what's actually going on. We have never learned that Flight or Fight is simply trying to come to our rescue, trying to get us away from what we've labeled as dangerous.

One final, important issue to get very clear about in this discussion: we do not, repeat not, have to be conscious of "what if?" thinking to activate Flight or Fight. This is so important it bears repeating: Flight or Fight will activate in the presence of anxious, "what if?" thinking, and it can happen as easily with thinking we're not conscious of as any conscious thought we experience.

A SYSTEM THAT'S GREAT FOR REAL, SERIOUS DANGER ISN'T SO GREAT WHEN WE'RE DEALING WITH ANXIOUS THINKING

To review, the impact of Flight or Fight on our bodies, our emotions and our thinking is utterly natural when we think we're in danger. Hopefully it's also clear that most or all of these reactions can be exceptionally helpful when we're dealing with actual danger.

But this book isn't about real danger. It's about the fight with anxiety and how that fight impacts our lives, as well as what we can actually do to get free of the debilitating effects of anxiety. It's one thing to have Flight or Fight fire up when we're trying to evade a drunk driver. It's something else entirely when the host of reactions Flight or Fight summons flare up when we are, as far as we can tell, just living our lives.

I have reviewed all this about Flight or Fight for three reasons:

1) Everything we experience in our Flight or Fight response is COMPLETELY NORMAL. There is absolutely nothing wrong with us when we have any of these reactions.

2) We trigger Flight or Fight when we perceive danger—whether it's real or exists only in our thinking.

3) We learn to start thinking of Flight or Fight responses as scary things all by themselves—when they are not.

Your body, emotions and mind are all impacted in a big way by the triggering of Flight or Fight. That's crucial if you're dealing with lions or drunk drivers. It is anything but useful if you're having scary thoughts, conscious or otherwise.

....

The only lasting, effective way to deal with anxiety is

to get at the core of the problem—which is the "what

if?" thinking we're doing that started this whole circus.

....

This theory of anxiety may seem to run counter to our own experience with anxiety. For many of us—perhaps most of us—the battle with anxiety came on us "out of the blue", with little warning and no clear origins. The next chapter deals with the origins of this anxious thinking in our lives, and it is useful to understand these origins as we move to the second goal of this book—a clear toolkit for dealing with and overcoming anxiety.

CHAPTER 3

The Origins of "What If?" Thinking

Nothing in life is to be feared, it is only to be understood. Now is the time to understand more, so that we may be fearless.
Marie Curie

S o far we've reviewed the way anxiety gets started in our thinking—by doing "what if?" thinking, treating an issue, problem or concern as a crisis—and the way Flight or Fight responds to that thinking, amplifying our worry with a desperate (and usually futile) effort to get us to safety.

Part of what makes this so crazy-making for we who fight or have fought anxiety is that in the beginning we usually don't have much (or any) warning when anxiety first parks itself on our doorstep. It all seems a big mystery, breeding a lot of misconceptions about what anxiety is and is not.

The goal of this chapter is to make crystal clear how anxious thinking gets set up in each of us, with the mission of dispelling as much mystery as possible. Anxiety doesn't "just come out of the blue." We learn to think anxiously.

WE HAVE TO LEARN TO THINK THIS WAY—LIKE WE LEARN MOST OF OUR THINKING

When I say "taught" I do not mean that somebody deliberately set out to make us anxious thinkers. What I mean is that we learned at the feet of people who themselves had anxious elements in their thinking—and we learned from both their example and our experience to do that type of thinking ourselves.

This is one vital piece of understanding about what it means to be a human being—that we are taught to think. A good metaphor might be this: our brains are our laptop or phone, and our thinking is the software that runs on that laptop or phone. We can have great laptops or phones, but they are only as useful as the programs/apps that we run on them.

The same can be said for our thinking. It is rarely the brain itself that is the problem when it comes to anxiety. The problem stems from the thinking we're doing with that brain.

Rarely, of course, does anyone learn to be ONLY an anxious thinker. Most of us think about some things as problems, and some things as crises. But it is when we begin thinking about an issue as a crisis that we run afoul of anxiety.

The specifics at this part of the discussion don't really matter. It might be about money management, or money in general. It might be about relationships, or making mistakes, or having the right career. It might be about appearing confident, capable and never at a loss. It could be about all those things and more.

The bottom line is that we're treating some issue as dangerous, even lethal, in our thinking. An example might be a person who grows up the daughter of a mom who sees safety as someone in her life she can lean on when she's in trouble—i.e., the absolute need for a "safe person" who can come to her rescue when she needs it.

If you grew up in that situation it would be easy to develop the same belief. This belief might never, ever be explicitly expressed out loud. It might only be communicated by example, by warning, by overheard conversations and by the assumptions that both the mother and child make about what constitutes safety.

....

In fact, the learning is all but invisible to the child. But it is no less learned because it is not explicitly taught.

But although it is not explicitly taught, it is no less learned, and this thinking is there in the background, coloring and shaping much of how we see our world.

....

So let's continue with the example of needing a "safe person." Our child, now an adult, assumes as gospel truth that she can't really make it in the world on her own. She has to have a go-to person in her life, someone who (although she might not ever say this out loud) she feels is competent to take care of themselves and other people.

Her "what if?" thinking might go like this: "What if I lose this person? What if I can't find someone to replace this person? What if I get too far away physically from this person and need help that I know I can't provide for myself? What if this person doesn't like me and won't help me because I drew a boundary, or asked for something they don't want?"

Heaven forbid the relationship is rocky, or the other person is also anxious. Notice in this discussion there was no intention, no malice on the part of the parent in passing along this pattern of anxious thinking to their child. It was simply trained up in the course of living.

And it isn't just family that can teach us to think in terms of "what if." We can learn it from multiple sources—school, friends, other family members, co-workers. Of course, our experience also plays a role, but that experience is usually building on "what if?" thinking that we've already learned to apply to that experience.

In a very real sense I'm pinning the blame for anxiety on an (unintentional) lack of good critical thinking skills. This is a difficult subject for many of us. We can get very defensive about the quality of our thinking. Part of this stems from our lack of understanding that thinking is something we learn, as opposed to something we naturally possess at birth.

In other words, to examine the quality of our thinking is not the same as saying we are failures or bad people because we don't think clearly or skillfully about something! To accuse someone of having a cold is not the same as saying they are somehow a failure for getting sick. It's just an observation, a fact we can use to deal with that cold and make it better.

And there may not be a more important thing to be objective and evaluative about than the skill and clarity of our thinking. Anxiety stems directly from how we think. To address anxiety effectively and decisively requires that we get clear about how we think about the things that make us anxious in the first place.

THE UNCONSCIOUS/SEMI-CONSCIOUS NATURE OF MUCH OF OUR THINKING

As if it weren't bad enough that we learn anxious thinking, we also have to deal with the fact that much of our thinking runs outside of our conscious awareness. This is an unfamiliar thought to many of us, at least in the sense that we can be actually thinking (as opposed to just, say, breathing, or having our heart beat) without being conscious of those thoughts.

Our brains are like a stage in a theater, with the house lights out and a single spotlight on the stage. Anything in that spotlight is visible and clear. Anything outside that spotlight is in the shadows, hard or even impossible to see until we turn the spotlight in that direction.

....

Just as on a stage, there can be a lot happening in our brains that isn't immediately visible to our conscious awareness. We can have powerful thoughts that fire up Flight or Fight, and not be aware that we've had these thoughts.

....

This is one of the primary reasons why people often report both that they don't know why they're anxious, and that anxiety must be something physically wrong. After all, they'd know if they had an anxious thought, wouldn't they?

Not necessarily. In fact we often, especially before we begin any deliberate work about our anxiety, don't have much conscious awareness at all about what is scaring us in our thinking. I'm not saying that we can't become conscious of the thinking that is making us anxious—just like anything on the stage can be illuminated by the spotlight. It is a matter of turning our attention to our fearful thinking, something that can be done with practice.

This will, of course, make us uncomfortable, very uncomfortable, scared and anxious. After all, we don't really want to think about our fears, and Flight or Fight will most definitely fire up as we turn to confront the thinking that has been making us miserable. That doesn't mean we can't do this confronting. This is work we can do, any of us.

WHAT IF? The Art of Crushing Anxiety

WHERE DOES ALL THIS LEAD?

I emphasize the learned and largely unconscious growth of anxious thinking in part to set up how anxiety tends to come upon most of us—i.e., how we first become aware that we have issues with anxiety at a conscious level. This can be, by itself, a very disturbing, scary and difficult dawning of awareness, and we can take away exactly the wrong ideas about what's happening to us.

At some point in our life we become aware to some extent that we are wrestling with a problem (or problems) that scares us. This might be as mild as a slow-growing sense that we are avoiding certain topics, or stalling on making important decisions. It might be a mild burst of anxiety when confronted by something we realize we've been scared of for longer than we've been consciously aware.

Or it might manifest itself in a full-blown panic attack, one that seems to come out of nowhere. Regardless of how our awareness starts most of us find ourselves frightened and unsure of what's going on. Given that most of us don't realize we're doing battle with "what if?" thinking, we make a variety of assumptions.

Some of us think we are losing our minds! And why wouldn't we? It seems like we are going OUT of our minds. Others think there must be something physically wrong—a tumor in our brains or a mysterious illness that makes us feel this way. Still others might assume it's just a one-time thing, and attempt to shrug it off, but find that they are now nervous this unexplained thing will happen again, and they are determined to avoid it.

Remember, it is the great mission of Flight or Fight to get us away from whatever is scaring us. The vast majority of us, faced with this mystery of anxiety manifesting in our bodies and thinking, pull back and work to avoid whatever we happened to be around when this flared up, in an effort to get away from it and not have it happen again.

....

Too often those of us who have a history of anxiety

are also somewhat disconnected from our bodies

and what they are trying to tell us. We're not really

comfortable with our physicality, and our bodies seem

like difficult and often mysterious machines that just

do things.

....

OK, so what do we know so far from this chapter? We know that:

- Anxiety doesn't just happen—we learn to think anxiously.
- This learning is usually transparent to us; we don't know we're learning it.
- We can learn it from multiple sources.
- It is essentially a gap in our thinking skills, and is one we can fix!
- It is often largely unconscious thinking.
- We didn't know what was going on while we were learning it; we just knew we were afraid.
- We often take the wrong messages away from our first conscious contacts with our anxiety. Instead of realizing

it's simply anxiety, we think we're going crazy, or there is something physically wrong with us.

What I hope you're clear about from this chapter is that anxiety is not a permanent, unfixable problem. **Anything we learn to think we can also learn to think differently.** Anxiety is rooted in our thinking, and our thinking is very much something we can change and modify.

That doesn't mean it's easy. It takes some serious work and effort over time. It is work anyone can do, but it's work. In the next chapter I will discuss a couple of important ideas: 1) the notion that we are rarely dealing with one fear at a time; 2) and the notion of habits in relation to thinking, and how those habits both make this changing of our thinking harder AND give us clear, achievable ways to change those habits into non-anxious thinking.

CHAPTER 4

The Tangle and the Habits

Thoughts crystallize into habit, and habit solidifies into circumstances.
Bryan Adams

Beyond the fundamentals of anxious thinking, there are a couple of other issues that serve to drive anxious thinking and make it more challenging to shift, at least at the outset. The first is that we are rarely dealing with just one anxious "what if?" thought at a time.

Thinking is an organic process. We don't think in nice, neat, linear ways. We don't just have one thought and then have another thought, one at a time. A good metaphor for the thinking process might be the roots of a plant or tree. They don't just grow in straight lines. They grow around each other, they weave in and out of each other, and they are usually a tangle.

Another good metaphor for our fearful thinking is a bowl of spaghetti. Our thinking is tangled, like the noodles. When we pull at one anxious "what if?" thought, we're more than likely to pull up two or three or four more anxious thoughts that are related.

Maybe the biggest reason it is important to grasp this tangled notion is that it can feel overwhelming—like all your fears are fighting for your attention right now. With Flight or Fight engaging (in response to our thinking) it becomes hard to think, and all we really want to do is get away from this thinking that scares us.

Multiple fears tangled together make for a daunting, if not deeply frightening, experience as we wade in and begin to make sense of our anxious thinking. I'll get to the details of that work in the toolbox section of this book. For the moment it's important to understand how organic our thinking is and how that organic nature makes this work messy, frustrating and scary.

It's one thing to think, for example, that I have been avoiding my fears of money management. It is something else to start to face those fears, only to also have my fear of being a failure in my career, my fear of never finding someone to love, and my fear of what other people will think of me when I'm living under a bridge (because I have no money, no career and no one to love) all come at me at the same time.

To add insult to injury, an anxiety fighter can wade into this work not understanding this notion of tangled anxious thoughts, and in the process, create fierce anxiety for him/herself. So much of this work to break the hold of anxiety is having a clear map of what is going on, and understanding what we can expect as we face down our fears. Not knowing what the hell is going on when our fears surface in our thinking can be by itself a frightening (and in this case, unnecessary) experience.

Part of what will help us in this tangle of "what if?" thoughts is remembering that it is ALL in our thinking—we are not actually facing real danger at the moment. Part of what will help is practicing the knowledge that how we feel is coming at us from Flight or Fight, which we have been firing up because we are scaring ourselves with "what if?" thinking. Part of what will help us is not trying to tackle all our fears at once, but taking them in pieces, and doing that work over time. I'll discuss this more as I move into the work of unpacking anxious thinking later in the book.

Tangled fearful thinking is one challenge. Another is the nature of habitual thinking and our need to understand how habits work in order to effectively deal with and change those habits.

THE NATURE OF HABIT AND ITS RELATION TO "WHAT IF?" THINKING

One of the things that has some direct use for those of us who fight or have fought chronic anxiety and depression is the concept of a habit. (For a great discussion of this subject check out *The Power of Habit* by Charles Duhigg.) Specifically, we anxiety fighters have developed what could accurately be called a small set of nasty habits. By understanding the precise nature of a habit, we can be more effective in both understanding the power of our "what if?" thinking AND effectively changing that thinking.

We all know what habits are, right? I know I thought I did. I thought a habit was simply a behavior pattern we are used to doing, one we don't think much about. If you had pressed me I might have added that habits have some payoff, historic or current—something that helps keep us doing them, even if it isn't always obvious what that payoff is.

Well, there's more to understand about habits. There are some very specific elements to habits that both make them more understandable and give us stronger tools to change habits we don't like. These tools can help us create habits we do want, and especially help us replace/rewrite the habit of chronic "what if?" thinking that make us crazed in the first place.

....

A habit is a piece of thinking we've "chunked" into

a single unit or routine in our brain. Think of it as a

small, automatic program that you (unintentionally,

most of the time) have set up in your thinking, like the

programs running on your computer.

....

Think of the example of brushing your teeth I mentioned in Chapter 1. What are all the specific steps involved in doing that task? You have to go into the bathroom, get your toothbrush, put some toothpaste on the brush, run some water to get that stuff wet, then run that brush repeatedly around the surfaces of your teeth. You do it for some period of time, then take the brush out of your mouth, rinse the toothpaste out, then maybe grab some floss and some mouthwash.

That's a lot of things to do in a row. But tell me, do you actually do much conscious THINKING around that process? No, of course not. You are in the grip of a little automatic program you're running while you think about the next day, or maybe how much you liked dinner tonight.

You're not thinking. You're just running that toothbrush program, a program we call a habit. Let's get more technical and more precise. You experienced a cue or stimulus. In this case, you had stuff stuck in your teeth, or the strong taste of garlic in your mouth, and so you started toward the bathroom. You ran your tooth-brushing program, then you got a reward for it—a tingling feeling in your mouth and no more stuff stuck in your teeth.

Cue, routine, reward. That's what makes up a habit. So how does this apply to our understanding of anxious, "what if?" thinking and the rush of Flight or Fight?

WHAT IF?—A NASTY HABIT

As I do coaching and group discussions around the work of overcoming anxiety, I am always telling people the core of the problem is our "what if?" thinking, where we turn problems into crises in our thinking and then ask ourselves frightening, terrible "what if?" questions about the outcomes. People usually tell me, "Sure, Erik, I buy it. I'm scaring myself in my thinking. But I don't really consciously know my 'what if?' thoughts. They seem hard to identify or pin down, which makes me think I'm NOT thinking 'what if?' thoughts."

That makes sense. As I've already discussed, we learned to do "what if?" thinking a long, long time ago. By the time 99 percent of us get to a place where we're aware that we are dealing with anxiety at all, that thinking has been "chunked" into a habit (really, multiple habits) and is running very much on automatic pilot in our skulls.

So we wouldn't necessarily BE aware of the habitual thinking we're doing. Let me make that stronger: when we start this work, and even when we're well into this work, we will have anxious thinking that is not conscious—at least not right away—and it will take work to make it conscious for ourselves. It might be a feeling as simple as when you first awaken in the morning and immediately feel terrible—sad, hopeless, upset, afraid, you name it. You report that you "just feel sad" or "woke up really anxious." You were not consciously aware of the thinking that made you feel that way, because that thinking is a habit chunk, a little program (or for most of us, several little programs) of scared, "what if?" thinking that has been running for years or even decades.

It zipped through your skull, maybe even before you were awake, and so you find yourself with all kinds of Flight or Fight reactions—feelings and physical sensations, and you think "Crap, here we go again. What is wrong with me?" What's wrong with you is your thinking habits—your "what if?" habits.

Habits only get set up when there is a payoff to the routine/program in response to the cue that starts the whole routine. What could possibly be a reward for getting caught up in scary thinking? Well, for starters, we don't set out to scare ourselves. We set out to solve a crisis, or at least a crisis that we're making out of a problem, a situation or challenge in our thinking. The cue is the crisis thinking. The routine is Flight or Fight doing what it is supposed to do, trying to find a way to escape from the crisis.

And the reward? There are a couple of possibilities. One is that worrying or agonizing over the future feels like we're doing something concrete and useful in the face of our fears. That this isn't useful 99 percent of the time is beside the point because it feels like it is useful. I probably can't overstate this point: feeling like something is useful is often more than enough to keep us persisting in that thing, regardless of how useful it actually is to us.

Another likely reward of that habit may be that sometimes in the past, worrying about something has given us a solution. It's a lot less often than we believe, but once in a while worrying over something seemed to bring an answer. That answer might have happened for several reasons: the problem resolved itself, you got some outside help, or even a wild-ass effort resulted in some answer to your "crisis" thinking. But there was a payoff in the problem being resolved in some way.

I bet you have experienced both of these rewards for worry. The bottom line is, the vast majority of our anxious thinking is a habit that's had just enough reinforcement to become a habit, regardless of whether it's a useful habit or not. And what happens as a result of 99 percent of our worried, anxious, fearful thinking? We simply strengthen that useless habit, and encourage it to continue.

THIS JUST IN: HABITS DON'T HAVE TO BE GOOD

These little automatic programs called habits are powerful things. And like it or not, we're going to create and have habits; it's a human thing. But here's some good news: we don't have to be slaves and helpless prisoners to our habits.

We can take command of our habits. We can learn to overwrite our old anxious thinking with new, problem-solving habits. I'll discuss this more in the toolbox section of this book, but for the moment it is useful to understand habits are both **persistent in nature** and **automatic in function.**

Understand this truth: we are not the forever prisoners

of our anxious thinking. It's simply habitual thinking

we need to change and overwrite. It can be done.

Automatic doesn't mean we're trapped or doomed.

A REMINDER OF HOW EARLY THIS STARTS FOR MOST OF US

As I mentioned in Chapter 3, we start learning these habits of anxious thinking very early. This is deeply embedded behavior, thinking patterns that were laid down and firmly entrenched in our brains years and years ago. It is this early training and habit-building that often makes it very hard for us to embrace the notion that we are suffering from a thinking problem, rather than something physical. After all, we've soldiered on for quite a while, and then suddenly (it seems) we're hit out of the blue with this truckload of anxiety. How could it have been there the whole time?

The answer depends on individual situations. Some of us get well into early adulthood, or later, before we have our first serious bout with anxiety. Others of us know in elementary school that we are in the grip of worry and fear. Some contributing factors may be how much stress we have in our immediate environments, how unstable our home situation is, the state of our physical health, and more.

Even the way in which anxiety impacts our lives varies enormously. While I am primarily writing this book to those of us who have fallen into the vortex of chronic or acute anxiety (more about that in Chapter 5) this applies to anyone who is dealing with ongoing anxiety around one or more issues.

We had to learn to think anxiously, and that learning began early for us. We've become very adept at working around our anxiety. Afraid to take plane trips? We find ways to travel on the ground, or not travel at all. Afraid to speak to a group of people at work? We'll go out of our way to find reasons why we can't do that. Scared to really sit and look at our personal finances? We'll let money issues get completely away from us, (spend too much or become absolute misers) rather than turn and look our fears in the eye.

And so our long retreat begins. Retreat long enough, get anxious enough, and we start to impact the quality of our lives. Keep at it and we begin to develop long-term symptoms of chronic anxiety, and have to start dealing with the havoc that anxiety can bring. I'll discuss this more in Chapter 5.

So, to recap this chapter:

- Fears usually travel in groups: we don't usually wrestle with one fear at a time.
- Fearful thinking is habitual thinking, formed over time, running unconsciously or semi-consciously in the background.
- We can learn to overwrite those old anxious thinking habits with new habits.
- This habitual thinking doesn't have to make a mess of us right away. We can become very adept at working around our fears, until one day they become too much for us to avoid.

The long-term outcomes of chronic, anxious thinking both muddy the water about what we're fighting and also make chronic anxiety so debilitating.

CHAPTER 5

Learned Helplessness, Long-term Results of Chronic Anxiety, and an Anxious View of the World

Habits of thinking need not be forever. One of the most significant findings in psychology in the last twenty years is that individuals choose the way they think.
Martin Seligman

We now have a foundation for understanding anxiety: what it is, where it comes from, how we get caught up in it, how it makes us feel.

This chapter is about some of the outcomes of chronic anxiety, such as panic attacks, inaccurate and often dangerous thinking about what anxiety actually is, and perhaps its most difficult and debilitating result, depression. To start this discussion, it is important to remember that most of us don't understand what is going on when we begin to realize we have a problem with anxiety. Even identifying it AS anxiety is elusive to many of us.

Remember, we learned early that there were one or more (usually more) issues, situations, problems that we should treat as a life-or-death crisis. Depending on how many issues we learned to see this way, how often we were confronted with those issues, and how much stamina we had to power through those problems-turned-crises in our thinking, we will have varying journeys on our way to chronic anxiety.

It is important to see anxiety as a progression, a road we walk. Some of us will start to experience chronic anxiety much earlier than others. Some of us might be well into adulthood before we have any idea that we're dealing with this anxiety thing. How does this journey develop and progress?

As mentioned in Chapter 4, we have developed these fierce habits of anxious thinking. We have little or no idea we've developed these habits, but they dominate our life in ways we're only, at most, peripherally aware of day-to-day. And, of course, every time we have an anxious thought zip through our thinking, we fire up Flight or Fight, and then we feel scared, anxious, worried, helpless.

This happens again and again some days. Other days we may be mostly or totally removed from what makes us anxious. We might call those days "good" days because we think we've gotten away from our anxiety. Then we're confronted with those issues again, those problems-turned-crises, and bam, we're back to reacting with anxious thinking and Flight or Fight.

So the cycle of anxiety continues. For some of us it may never get much worse. We have one or two or three areas in our lives that we're doing "what if?" thinking about, but it never really progresses much further than that. For many others one result of that habitual anxious thinking might be called a long retreat. We begin to flinch away, more and more, from our anxiety, and whatever we associate with our anxiety. That retreat can continue for years or decades before we slide into chronic anxiety.

In a sense, with that retreat, we start backing ourselves into a corner. The corner might take a long time to reach (and does, for some of us) but eventually we run out of retreating room. As we begin to run out of mental and emotional room to run (because of course we're not actually running away from real danger, just the danger we've conjured in our fearful, "what if?" thinking) our anxiety begins to escalate.

This is about the time many of us begin fighting panic attacks—another outcome of long-term anxiety. Panic attacks might be described as overload reactions to anxiety, anxiety carried too long without being addressed in useful ways.

Panic attacks are in reality not dangerous. They feel terrible—awful—like the world coming to an end. They feel exactly like we are about to be eaten by a tiger. Rational thought is in short supply (note: not completely out of reach, but in short supply) and all we want is to RUN.

Panic attacks are great indicators that we've reached the edge of our capacity for anxiety/stress/worry, and we need to do something about it (besides run, that is). They are also the way our body can dump all the stress hormones that have been cascading through our body from the anxious thinking and reacting we've been doing.

But they are not dangerous. It may feel like we're dying, but we're just suffering through a very strong anxiety response. Please know that I'm not trying to minimize how these attacks feel. They were among the worst experiences of my life. I am, however, working very hard here to help you understand that they are just symptoms; they don't mean anything except that a person is dealing with a tremendous amount of stress in their thinking. They can't hurt us.

Of course, there is no one path in our retreat from anxiety. We might have panic attacks early in our lives. I had my first one in junior high school. We might have a series of panic attacks, and then find life returns to "normal" (free of obvious evidence of chronic anxious thinking). That "normal" state can exist for years, until our "what if?" thinking spikes again, and our anxiety escalates to a severe state.

It is also possible to not have a panic attack of note until our twenties or thirties. Some people never have a full-blown panic attack. They just suffer under a tremendous burden of anxiety, never quite tipping over into that particular long-term outcome to anxiety.

The apparently erratic nature of this progressive development of anxiety can lead to another difficult symptom of chronic anxiety—inaccurate explanations for what is happening to us. That may sound like a strange symptom, but it is important to understand that we are, too often, operating on some terrible assumptions about what is and isn't possible to do about anxiety.

And why would we know any better? This strange anxiety stuff seems to come out of nowhere, and worse, seems to come and go with no clear predictable pattern. Sure, we know that some things make us feel anxious, but even those seem to have more or less impact on us from day to day, year to year.

The "just anxious" assumption puts the blame on some mysterious flaw in us as people. Some people infer that this means anxiety is inheritable—i.e., there is some genetic issue with anxiety. This is very murky territory, for multiple reasons. That there are conditions that can make someone more prone to becoming anxious seems clear these days from current genetics research.

For instance, to be an anxiety fighter requires a pretty solid brain: intelligence is required. You have to be good at extrapolating the future and able to engage in abstract thoughts about what might be, what might happen someday. Yeah, I'm saying that smart people are more prone to anxiety.

Another trait appears to be a slightly higher than average sensitivity to the world around us—things like light and noise and general agitation. (For a longer discussion on these points see *Free From Fears,* referenced in the bibliography of this book.)

But those traits don't by themselves make us anxious. It is still "what if?" crisis thinking that starts us down the road to chronic anxiety.

....

The idea that we are predisposed to be more at risk

for anxious thinking if we learn to think anxiously

is worlds away from saying that we are doomed by

genetics to be anxious.

....

Let me say it again: anxiety is a thinking problem. We are not born with our thinking tendencies. We learn them as we go along. We have the hardware—our brains. We have to acquire the software—our thinking patterns, assumptions and beliefs.

I drive this discussion so hard because some of us find it very easy to say, "Oh, well, I'm just an anxious person," as if anxiety were a personality trait that we are given at birth. Not so, and also not useful. It's too easy to default to giving up if you think you're naturally doomed to anxiety.

Another theory of anxiety is that there is something fundamentally wrong with one or more of our neurotransmitters, with the usual suspect being serotonin. Certainly serotonin is impacted by a number of variables, and there is definitely evidence that says that reduced serotonin levels are found in people who are dealing with chronic anxiety.

But this only begs the question: which comes first—reduced serotonin levels or anxious thinking? I am no neurologist, but there is good evidence that chronic anxious thinking (and the resulting Flight or Fight reactions in our bodies and brains) can impact serotonin levels—specifically, slowly reducing them over time, leaving us with lowered thresholds to stimuli, making us more prone to Flight or Fight firing up.

This means that if we begin to tackle that anxious thinking, reducing the tendencies to generate "what if?" thoughts and the resulting fright responses, we can take serotonin levels in the opposite direction. Once anxious, always anxious (the idea that we can manage anxiety but never be free of chronic anxiety) simply isn't true.

I'm not saying it doesn't FEEL that way. Part of this belief, I suspect, stems from how little we understand how dense and quick our anxious thinking can become active in the background of our thinking. We've been fighting it for years and decades, we've tried different things—desensitization, medications, meditation, etc. But because we didn't understand this fundamental truth of anxiety—that it is based in anxious thinking—nothing changed for us.

....

Don't take my word for any of this, by the way.

Everything I advocate, in this work of breaking the

hold of anxious thinking, is MEANT to be road-tested.

....

Either of these assumptions can lead us to a third notion—that the only way we're going to ever feel "normal" or have a life is to treat our anxiety forever with some form of medication.

There's no question that when used correctly medication can be a tool that can assist us in this fight. Meds can, for some people, ease the impact of Flight or Fight reactions to anxious thinking. Flight or Fight is show-stopping scary for the vast majority of us, and in easing that roar of sensations and feelings we can get better clarity in our thinking.

But that isn't the same thing as saying we can only find relief with meds. In fact, as I'll outline in Chapter 6, in the final analysis, medication can't end the reign of anxiety in our lives **by itself.** Do not infer from this that meds aren't useful. Please read chapter 6 to get a clear understanding of the role of medication in this work.

In summary, given our lack of understanding or information about what is going on when we feel seriously anxious, we can wind up with assumptions about anxiety that are just not helpful. And worse, these assumptions can seriously interfere with our getting over anxiety.

The third outcome of chronic anxiety is depression. Lots of people see anxiety and depression as two very different things—but the vast majority of the time, they are not.

This notion that depression could be an outcome of anxiety was brilliantly demonstrated in a series of experiments conducted at the University of Pittsburgh back in the 1960's. Martin Seligman, a research psychologist and the author of books including *Authentic Happiness,* describes the following experiment: A dog was put into a wire cage. The bottom of the cage was electrified (the person running the experiment could run an electric shock through the cage bottom). The dog was secured in the cage, and then shocked again and again. Then the cage door was opened and the dog was shocked again. In addition, there was food or a treat outside the cage, and the assumption was made that the dog, both seeing his/her freedom and smelling the food/treat, would take the first opportunity to leave the cage. To the researcher's surprise (and our great gain in understanding) the dog DIDN'T leave the cage.

Why? The door was open, it really could leave, so what was the problem? The problem, as it turned out, was that the dog had tried to escape, frequently, earlier in the experiment. Of course it did—it was getting shocked! But after trying a number of times and failing it gave up, lay down and suffered through more shocks.

There is a happy ending to this story. The dogs were taught they could leave the cage, and they did leave. I know this may sound like the worst sort of sadistic torture, but believe me, not only did it teach us something hugely important, but the dogs were not hurt long-term.

Another good piece of news is that we learned something about living creatures in general, including human beings. We learned that we can literally learn to give up, something that is now called learned helplessness. There's another name for this giving up: depression.

WE CAN TAKE ENOUGH INJURY/SETBACKS/ANXIETY TO TEACH US (INCORRECTLY) THAT THERE IS NO POINT IN TRYING.

So we stop trying, either for periods of time or worse, forever. As bad as things are, we assume they can't get better. We've tried before, tried and tried, but nothing worked. So we learn to expect that nothing WILL work—that there isn't any point, and we should just give up.

Entirely too many of us have been fighting this whole fear/anxiety/worry thing for a LONG time—years, even decades. We have had a kind of vampire at our throats, sucking the life out of us. As I said in Chapter 4, the mostly or completely unconscious habits of anxious thinking are the root cause. Like the dog in the cage, if we've been at this long enough we may wind up feeling hopeless.

We don't have to stay there. I can try to break a padlock all I want—but unless I have a big steel hammer I'm unlikely to succeed. There is however one other option—I could find the key. Anxiety is a great deal like that padlock. We can want to open the lock—we can shout and batter and bruise ourselves trying to open it—but in the end it really is about finding a useful key.

Or, in this case, a small handful of skills. Those are coming in the toolbox section of this book. First, though, let's talk about how this hopelessness manifests in us. It has to run the gamut from anxiety through anger to what we call depression. We have to understand that depression, by and large, is a long-term outcome to chronic anxiety.

WHERE DEPRESSION FITS IN THE EVOLUTION OF ANXIETY

In talking about anxiety and its cousin depression, it is useful to understand that anxiety is really two things: it is the thinking that scares us in the first place AND the emotional reaction that we label "anxiety." The root cause is that thinking, pure and simple. We cannot and will not break the hold of anxiety in our lives until our thinking changes. End of story.

But anxious thinking doesn't constitute the entire problem. Flight or Fight, firing up in our brains and bodies in response to that anxious thinking, is what sends us running for the hills and experiencing all the emotional and physical drama that too often travels with anxious thinking.

A little review here: remember that Flight or Fight always starts with an effort to get away from the danger we are experiencing, if we're actually in a real, life-or-death crisis or if we think we're in a crisis (engaging in anxious thinking). It's invariably better in the natural world to run away from danger, because if we succeed then hey, no injury, no damage, and we live to run away another day. Running makes sense in the natural world when real danger shows up, and it is carved into our very genes, into the alarm system called Flight or Fight.

....

That running away feeling is what we call anxiety.
Anxiety says, "Holy crap, this is scary as hell! I'd better
get my frightened self outta here." This is why your
cat jumps eight feet in the air when you surprise it.

....

And this is why you get that anxious, restless, let's-get-moving urge whenever you are confronted by one of your fearful thoughts—when you are troubled by sensations or feelings from Flight or Fight, and you're not necessarily conscious of your anxious thinking.

Of course, the vital thing to be clear about is the difference between REAL, life-or-death danger and the perceived, in-our-thinking nature of our fear from anxious thinking. **They are not the same and can't be treated the same.**

Anxiety = running. Great. Except in the natural world we sometimes can't get away from the thing or experience that is threatening us. Sometimes we have no choice but to fight.

ANGER—ANXIETY'S FIRST COUSIN

When we are physically or mentally trapped and can't exercise the option of running (at least not yet), we escalate to anger. Again, this makes a lot of sense in the natural world. ANY creature will fight if cornered, because if it's really life-or-death, then fighting is the only option.

This can take a couple of forms in the natural world. This can be full-out confrontation—a fight between predator and prey, a fight between natural enemies—but it can happen whenever a creature feels threatened and assumes that there is no other way to get what they need; they can't run from that situation without threatening their survival.

This is why when you reach to get that piece of steak that fell on the floor away from your dog or cat, it might growl or hiss at you. You're threatening its survival, after all. This is why every creature, including even advanced, big-brained humans, gets angry, defensive, even growls when we think someone is threatening our survival.

We can feel every bit as trapped by our anxious thinking as well. Here's an example: let's say we avoid thinking about managing our money. I was terrified for years and years of dealing directly with my money/finances. Maybe your direct deposit goes straight to your checking account, and you only even get close to seeing your balance when you go to the ATM to grab some cash. Otherwise you artfully glance away from the bottom-line total in your account. In essence, you run away from the "danger" of the anxious thinking around money/finances.

So far so good, at least as far as not dealing with your anxiety. But then you get a note from the bank that says, "Hey, knucklehead, your account is overdrawn! Give us some money!" Now you HAVE to deal with your bank account and the whole money issue. Ugh! No! Now you get pissed off. Maybe you stomp around the house. Maybe you yell at your kids. Maybe you start crying from sheer frustration. But whatever you do, you're mad.

....

You're angry because you feel threatened but you

can't run away. You have to fight this fight until the

threat stops for you.

....

In other words, anger becomes, "Holy crap, I'm being threatened and I can't run. I have to fight, at least until I win the fight or an avenue for running opens up." Anger = fighting, until the threat ends or you CAN run.

Some of us have learned to see anger as this uncontrollable, out-of-nowhere monster that can ruin our days and mess up our relationships and lives. Some of us think anger is its own creature, a wild animal that we have to cage away and control. Not true.

Anger is anxiety that feels like it can't escape, and produces the feeling that fighting WILL bring relief/ freedom from risk. It doesn't HAVE to be conscious.

These are deeply embedded reactions, natural to us. But the thinking that lies behind those anxious and angry responses can be addressed, cleaned up, and set to rights.

DEPRESSION—ANXIETY'S SECOND COUSIN

There is one more member of the anxiety family: depression. Here's the summary: depression is essentially "I'm feeling threatened but I can't run and I can't fight. There's nothing I can do."

Depression is an outcome of long-term anxiety. But that explanation misses the gut punch of depression—the conviction that there is no hope, no future, that all options have been closed off and this, whatever this is, will never change, and this is bad.

Wrong. What we're labeling as a crisis in our thinking isn't the monster we've made it into over a period of time. Depression for most of us springs from a long history of being anxious. As long as we think there is some way out, even via avoidance, then anxiety stays anxiety. Anxiety tips to depression when the sense of being trapped begins.

This is a thinking thing. It is strongly amplified by Flight or Fight. But make no mistake: if we are not actually trapped in a cage, then we are not trapped. Our beliefs, fears, rules, faiths, assumptions may leave us believing we are trapped, but we're not.

One more thing to get clear on: depression is a transient state much of the time. Much of our depression is a thing of the afternoon, or 20 minutes, or two days, or constant dipping into depression and then back out to chronic anxiety. Why do I mention this? Because again, we are NOT trapped, and we are not doomed. The only way that happens is if we can't see through to the anxious thinking that is making us depressed in the first place.

We are not dogs trapped in cages. We feel like that, but that feeling is a product of Flight or Fight, reacting to the conviction that we're facing a crisis we can't escape from, rather than a problem in the way we are thinking that we need to address and do something about.

I know what it's like to have to fight serious depression. "It sucks" only begins to describe how ugly and debilitating everything is when we're depressed. The world goes black, the joy seems to evaporate from living, nothing seems interesting, and it is an effort just to go through the motions of daily living.

Even simple things like taking a shower or eating a meal (let alone preparing that meal) seem like an enormous challenge when you're in the throes of depression. It is even hard to remember when things were better. It seems ridiculous to consider that things will improve, regardless of what other people tell you or however much they work to comfort you or cheer you up.

Please be clear: I am NOT minimizing the impact of depression in our lives. I am, however, saying that in most cases it has clear origins, it isn't a mystery and it can be dealt with directly by dealing with our anxious thinking. In the toolbox section of this book you'll find the tools you can use to apply this to your own life, and see the result for yourself.

TOO MANY OF US ARE ANXIOUS AND DEPRESSED

I've read varying numbers, but it looks like anywhere between 9 percent and 15 percent of people in the U.S. deal with depression in various forms every year. That's a lot of people wrestling with depression. And those numbers only reflect the people who have actually sought out help or are willing to tell a survey person they are wrestling with depression. While there obviously isn't any data on those folks, I'm willing to bet at least another 10 percent to 15 percent of us fall into the silent sufferers category.

Here's another challenge with the subject of depression; it is seen as a character flaw, a weakness. The prevailing attitude seems to be that we should be able to manage it ourselves without help.

This leads to way too many people who work to hide their depression, or explain it away as something other than depression, or worse, find their own ways to medicate it, with alcohol, drugs, eating, shopping. You name it, and the human race has tried to use it as a way to combat depression.

Anxiety can sometimes seem like a skillful actor—or maybe disguise artist. Sometimes it is crystal clear to us that we are in the grip of anxiety/fearful thinking. But sometimes anxiety wears other masks, and in doing so can muddy the water, confusing us as to why we're feeling what we are feeling, and what we should or can do about it.

Anxiety is particularly good at making us give up, just stop trying, if we think we are dealing with something we can't change. These inaccurate beliefs/assumptions are especially insidious when it comes to getting us to give up, and that isn't useful.

Maybe the best way to map this anxiety thing is to see it as a story we've learned to tell ourselves over time. It isn't a story we started really writing ourselves—it was a story about how to see the world that we learned largely from other people in our lives.

That story, however, grew and expanded until we came to see too much of the world as a crisis to resolve, instead of a problem to address and work through. As that story took over great chunks of our thinking, Flight or Fight became a too-constant companion.

Worst of all, we didn't really understand it was a story at all. We thought it was truth, who we were, how life just "was," and we began to feel more and more trapped in our lives. Stories are mental things, things we build, expand on, refine and see the world through. It's time for a different story—a much more accurate, reality-reflecting story about what anxiety is and what we can do about it. In the next chapter, I'll review where medication—and the behavior of medicating—fits in this map of anxiety, and what we can do about it.

CHAPTER 6

The Role of Medication (and Medicating) in Dealing with Anxiety

Medicine is not only a science; it is also an art. It does not consist of compounding pills and plasters; it deals with the very processes of life, which must be understood before they may be guided.
Paracelsus

The subject of medication is a difficult one. Enormous numbers of anxiety fighters depend on medication as the single bulwark between them and their fear.

Medication is the go-to solution for most physicians when they hear their patients say, "I think I'm anxious." The number of anti-anxiety and anti-depression prescriptions in this country looks like this: one in six Americans take some sort of psychiatric drug (www.livescience.com/57170-americans-psychiatrics-drug-use). It seems the medical community in general believes the only real solution to anxiety is medication in some form, and it's understandable why they might think that way. But while medication can provide relief—for some people, years of relief—it cannot and will not deal with the cause: anxious thinking.

MEDICATIONS CAN HELP

Let's be clear: medication can have an important and effective role in helping us break the hold of anxiety in our lives. Medication can, if used correctly, lessen the grip of Flight or Fight reactions in our body, which in turn can give us some useful room to think more clearly. This can give us the energy and breathing space to tackle our fearful thinking more effectively—give us a little more courage and some hope and fortitude in the tedium of this work.

It is my argument (and experience) that this is the thing medication can do. Medication cannot by itself change or correct anxious, "what if?" thinking. It is an excellent thing, make no mistake. Getting relief, any relief from the long-term effects of anxious thinking, is something most anxiety fighters would kill for.

But there are other issues with medication. Too many of us, not understanding anxiety in the first place and only wanting it to stop, turn to medication as the be-all/end-all of how we deal with anxiety. Most of us don't set out to do this, but over time medication can become a crutch and a way to avoid dealing with our anxious thinking. In finding some relief from the torment of feelings and physical reactions, we can continue to run away from the thinking that scares us, avoiding the work and letting the meds take the worst of the panic and worry away.

FIRST THINGS FIRST

If that's the case, what IS the role of medication in dealing with anxiety? Well, first we have to get clear that our primary mission is to get our thinking straightened out. If we are afraid, we have converted one or more problems into what we believe is a crisis. We have started down the rabbit hole of chronic anxiety and our thinking, in a very real sense, is spiraling out of control in the direction of our fears.

So the mission of medication has to be concerned with helping us cut that spiral, as well as assist in getting our thinking clear, useful, and effective. The effectiveness of this help will vary from person to person based on several factors. One is how severely anxious and/or depressed they are. Another is how they respond to a particular medication, both in how effective that medication proves for them and what side effects that medication may generate for them. In addition, many people begin to develop a tolerance for a particular medication, diminishing how effectively that medication continues to work for them.

What this means is that people can have widely varied responses to the same medication. A person can try one med and have excellent to moderate success with it, or they can run through a number of medications before finding one that makes a difference.

....

Medication isn't a miracle cure. Medication can do

good work, but let's be clear what we mean by work.

Can medication help us get some breathing room

from our thinking and Flight or Fight responses?

Very often the answer is yes. Can it end anxiety all by

itself? No.

....

But whatever people do experience with those meds, they in all likelihood won't shake free of anxiety until they sort out the thinking that makes them anxious in the first place. That's to be expected, and it DOESN'T mean we're doomed to keep feeling anxious/having anxiety run our lives.

The best research available says that meds work best in combination with some form of talk therapy. I will discuss the role of therapy in overcoming anxiety in Chapter 14 more fully, but for this chapter the bottom line is when they work effectively, meds give us the breathing room to do the hard work of sorting out our anxious thinking, which is what a therapist is trained to do.

ISSUES WHEN CONSIDERING THE USE OF MEDICATIONS

Meds are not as simple as starting one and finding relief. Some people experience fierce side effects with anti-anxiety and anti-depression medications. The side effects by themselves can either be disheartening in the work of beating anxiety, or they can create their own problems. Some of the side effects for anti-anxiety meds are nausea, headaches, sleepiness. More intense side effects include nightmares, dizziness, difficulty in thinking or remembering, and increased anxiety or depression (**www.nimh.nih.gov/health/topics/mental-health-medications/index.shtml**).

I don't spell out these issues of medications to scare anyone away or diminish what medication can potentially do. It is, however, very important to understand that medication, really any medication, is a matter of some experimentation, and should only be started under the care of a doctor. It is also important to understand that even if the medications do work, they can still bring some of these side effects.

As if this weren't enough, many people wrestle with the withdrawal effects that are part and parcel of coming off some medications. While those effects vary, perhaps the most difficult is how often withdrawal intensifies anxiety, depression, or both for some people, including physical and emotional Flight or Fight reactions that can be very debilitating (**www.psychcentral.com/blog/withdrawal-from-psychiatric-meds-can-be-painful-lengthy/**).

It is important to make the discussion of the role of medication in dealing with anxiety as transparent and honest as possible. When used well, and in conjunction with an effective therapist and under the care of the prescribing doctor, medication can be very helpful during the rough times in the work of cleaning up our thinking. It is important to that work to understand how meds work and the limitations of those medications.

It's been troubling over the past few years to hear coaching clients, my blog subscribers, friends and co-workers say things like, "Yeah, I've fought anxiety for a long time, but you know

Erik, I tried medication. It helped for a while (or a little, or not at all), but nothing really seemed to fix the problem. So I just don't think that it does any good to take meds. I'm just stuck with being anxious/depressed."

Yikes! When I hear people tell me things like this I have several concerns. Making a statement like that too often means this person has given up. They believe that they will have to endure anxiety for the rest of their lives. Ugh and double ugh—nothing could be further from the truth. I believed that for a long time. It was scary as hell, and it also shut me down from finding out whether or not that was actually the case.

It also makes me wonder about their experience with therapy and medication. Did they do therapy? Did they know they had more than one medication option? What were their assumptions about medication and therapy? What were their assumptions that got in the way, like the assumption they are untreatable, that their anxiety or depression was different/unique, or because one med or therapist didn't work out ALL meds and therapists are useless to them?

These folks are missing out on potentially powerful tools in their fight with anxiety. And there isn't any reason they need to do that. Just because meds and/or therapy haven't worked for them in the past doesn't necessarily mean they can't use those tools effectively, with a little knowledge and correct application.

DO THE HOMEWORK

Medication can have a role to play in breaking the hold of anxiety in our thinking. It is certainly something to consider as a tool, used correctly. There's no question that if you feel like you're at the end of your rope, you should see a doctor or a therapist and get some counsel on the use of medication to give you some breathing room.

....

> If something isn't working for you, tell your doctor or
>
> therapist, and be an advocate for yourself with the
>
> person you're working with. At the end of the day
>
> we are each responsible to understand the pros and
>
> cons of medication as they relate to and work for us.
>
> We have to do some learning for ourselves, and not
>
> simply depend on what one or another person tells us.

....

You may find medication is something you don't tolerate well. Or it could mean that you simply don't get much relief with medication. All of these things are possibilities. That doesn't mean you're doomed to be anxious for the rest of your life! It simply means you need to get into the work of unpacking your thinking and facing down your fears, with all the help you can get. More about that in the next chapters.

Remember, anxiety and depression make giving up and surrendering a very attractive, very easy thing to do. Too often, it feels like the only thing we can do. Remember, this is a thinking problem, amplified by Flight or Fight. It's time to start seeing anxiety for what it is, and to begin challenging the assumptions you've been carrying about your fear all this time.

You are not alone. You are not a freak, or damaged, or unable to break the hold of anxiety in your life, regardless of how you feel. There are resources and tools. Anxiety is not an invincible opponent. You can get free of anxious thinking. In the next chapter I outline the small handful of skills we all need to deal with anxiety effectively.

CHAPTER 7

The Four Skills of Fear Mastery

Knowledge is of no value unless you put it into practice.
Anton Chekhov

With this chapter I begin the discussion of the toolbox needed to get clear of the anxiety running our lives. This is not a complex thing, but it is very much a set of skills that takes practice, time and patience to acquire.

Here's some really good news: we can stop running. It will feel scary, sometimes very scary, to even consider that we can cease retreating and instead look our fears in the eye, but it is something we can do. It is in fact the thing we must do, because if we don't face down our fearful thinking, if we don't start challenging the problems we've turned into crises, we will continue to retreat from our lives. Our lives will continue to shrink, as too many of us already know from our own experience.

Here are the four skills needed to do this work effectively:

1. Identifying crisis thinking.
2. Learning to discount Flight or Fight's importance/ meaning.
3. Converting crisis thinking to problem thinking.
4. Learning self-care.

Each of these skills will get a longer and more complete discussion in the chapters that follow, but here is a brief overview of each.

Please see this model as just that—a model that gives shape to what is in reality a very organic, and often tangled, set of thoughts and responses. Life is rarely as clean as any model might make it seem, but models help us understand cause and effect enough to get our arms around a process.

SKILL 1: IDENTIFYING CRISIS THINKING

We have a thought, an issue, a concern, that we've learned over time to treat as a crisis. Sadly, 90 percent of the time, we don't understand we're treating that thought/issue/concern as a crisis. We are just reacting to it, treating it as truth.

The first step is to identify where we are treating issues, problems and concerns as crises. This is not as easy as it sounds. One issue that gets in the way is the tendency to flinch away from what scares us. We get very, very skillful at skipping over and walling away the thinking that frightens us, and it often takes real work and practice to "stay in the room" long enough to face that thinking and see it for what it is.

Another issue that slows this first step is lack of clarity. We will often find we identify a fearful "what if?" thought, only to realize with more work that it is actually another fear, or several other fears, that were "hiding" behind the first fear. This is an evolutionary and piecemeal process that takes time and repeated practice.

Finally, we are dealing with the sheer force of habit, long years (for most of us) of treating this issue, whatever it is, as a thing that's about to eat our face off. That's a fair amount of stuff to deal with as we start this work. We can do it, no doubt, but it can feel overwhelming for a stretch of time as we begin to practice our skills. And of course, at the core of those feelings is Flight or Fight.

SKILL 2: LEARNING TO DISCOUNT FLIGHT OR FIGHT'S IMPORTANCE/MEANING

When we start to turn and face our fearful thinking, we will also summon that guardian of our safety, Flight or Fight. It is my experience that most anxiety fighters are as terrified of their Flight or Fight reactions as they are of the thinking that starts Flight or Fight in the first place.

And why wouldn't we be scared as hell? Everything in our bodies and emotions seems to be shouting we're about to die—at least when we're truly scared. When Flight or Fight roars to life, it's hard to understand or keep in mind this isn't really true—that we are not about to die.

Yet skill #2 in this work is precisely this: understanding that we are only dealing with Flight or Fight. This is easy to say, but difficult to drive into our thinking and reacting. But it IS something we can learn to do. And in doing this we gain a control and freedom that we wouldn't dream possible while living with the fears of ongoing anxiety.

The bottom line is that this is all "what if?" thinking about our fears AND our Flight or Fight reactions. I call this out as distinct in this list of skills for two reasons. It is one thing to intellectually and abstractly see that we are scaring ourselves with our "what if?" thinking. Lots of us make some headway fairly quickly on this notion. But it is something else to stand in the torrent of feelings and sensations, especially those we've learned to treat as certain evidence of disaster, and practice seeing Flight or Fight reactions as only Flight or Fight reactions, not danger. Many anxiety fighters stall out here. Or worse, they decide how they feel must be real—otherwise why would they feel so strongly?

Another reason to emphasize this skill is that we are so darn ignorant of what's actually happening when we're in the grip of Flight or Fight. Our ignorance contributes to our anxiety in many ways, and in particular to our panicked reactions to our panic responses (physically, mentally and emotionally). With practice, there is no better weapon than good information in our fight to get free of the tyranny of anxiety.

Bottom line: learning to treat Flight or Fight as what it is—a reaction to anxious thinking, and not real danger—is a powerful tool in our hands.

SKILL 3: CONVERTING CRISIS THINKING TO PROBLEM THINKING

Learning to translate our anxious, "what if?" crisis thinking into problem thinking is at the very heart of this work. With this skill we decisively break the hold of anxiety in our lives. We will still get anxious, of course; anxiety is one of the tools we use to deal with situations that concern us. But with this skill even partly learned, anxiety will no longer be able to rule or ruin our lives.

For example, if we see lack of money as a crisis, then we are naturally going to react to money shortages AS a crisis, and scare ourselves silly around this issue. If we have told ourselves that being alone is the worst thing ever—that it's terrible, awful, and a signal that we are unlovable or unworthy of other people's time—then we are going to react to that experience as a crisis.

For the 95 percent of the time that we treat something as a crisis, we are taking the advice of Flight or Fight and running away from it. But as I said way back in Chapter 1, unless something is about to kill or maim us right here right now, then that something isn't a crisis.

This is really a reorientation of our thinking, and weirdly enough we already do it—at least about other things in our lives. Nobody treats everything they think about as a crisis. Of course, we can't get to this place if we don't first identify where in our thinking we're treating an issue as a crisis. And it can be very hard to treat something that is really a problem (not a crisis) as a problem if we're still freaking ourselves out with our anxious thinking and firing up Flight or Fight. This is why I have these skills in this order, even though we are usually working on all four skills at the same time, to some degree.

We won't make this leap instantly. We learned to think anxiously across a pretty serious span of time—for many of us, we did this for most of our lives right up until we begin this work. It will feel weird, even wrong and risky, to begin to make this shift in our thinking.

After all, lack of money really is a crisis, right? Well, no. It could eventually reach the place where we are in pretty dire straits, but 99 percent of us won't instantly starve to death or be evicted because we're short on cash. In fact, the real risk comes from treating this issue, or any other issue, as a crisis, because then we're usually not dealing with it effectively, or even at all. We're running from it, hiding from it, medicating to forget about it—anything but actually dealing with it.

SKILL 4: LEARNING SELF-CARE

Looming in the background of the development of these three skills is a fourth essential ability: the skill to take good, fundamental care of ourselves. Self-care will contribute to the success of our work in breaking anxiety's hold, and can even connect directly to our fearful, anxious thinking in a helpful feedback loop.

One aspect of self-care is physical maintenance. It is no secret that most of us are taking terrible care of ourselves in one or another aspect of our lives. There is nothing complex about this level of self-care: eating regularly and with some minimal thought to the quality of that food, working to get decent sleep to the extent we can, and engaging in regular physical movement and activity.

Let me be clear here. I'm not insisting that overcoming anxiety requires that we develop perfect sleep habits, become first-class athletes, or only eat organic food. Anxiety has a tedious way of taking everything to the extreme, and I've had more than one coaching client hear only extremes when I am simply recommending the most basic of self-care skills.

I am saying that we have to give some conscious thought to these basic needs if we're going to have the stamina and the capacity to see this work through. It's remarkable how even a limited quantity of decent sleep can help us think more clearly, including our work to clean up our anxious thinking. Everyone has had the experience of feeling better after just a short 15- to 20-minute walk, including clearer thinking and some improved energy. I'm not talking extremes here; I'm talking basics.

There is another level to this discussion of self-care. It is more advanced and for many of us, more challenging to do. It is learning to draw effective boundaries in our lives, deciding where we end and other people begin, and what works for us about our limits. Given how much anxiety many of us link to any form of saying no, or declining to leap to help someone the nanosecond they ask for it, drawing boundaries can be a very challenging skill to learn. It is also essential. Just the notion that we have limits, and that we have to learn to respect them, as well as to enforce them in some situations, is a brand new way of thinking for too many anxiety fighters.

....

It is also one of the most insidious energy drains I

know, this tendency in anxious people to believe that

EVERYONE comes before them, and to constantly

worry about "being selfish" if they even consider

treating themselves, at least sometimes, as well as

they treat other people.

....

You'll notice the repeated use of the word skill throughout this book, and particularly in this chapter. None of what I'm talking about here is anything magical, mysterious or beyond the reach of any human being. It is a combination of skills, learned over time and in the face of the reactions of Flight or Fight, that gives us the tools we need to escape the unintentional but self-created prison of relentless anxiety.

In the next five chapters I will dive into these skills in depth, provide examples of the work and explain how to apply what you're learning here.

CHAPTER 8

Identifying Crisis, "What If?" Thinking

We cannot solve problems by using the same kind of thinking we used when we created them.
Albert Einstein

The first skill we need to develop to get anxiety and fear out of the driver's seat of our life is getting clear on where we are converting problems to crises.

As I mentioned in Chapter 1, crisis thinking is the assumption that this issue, this problem, this challenge, if not addressed *immediately*, will kill or maim us. Anything else is a problem.

We evolved to respond quickly, effectively and immediately to life-threatening moments. In this book that's what I call a "crisis." This is exactly why Flight or Fight powers up: we tell it we're facing a life-or-death threat, and Flight or Fight leaps to the work of getting us ready to defeat it. This wonderful system developed to deal with real-world dangers—things that could hurt or kill us right now. Flight or Fight is our defense against tangible, physical danger. We are hard-wired for it, and if we see something dangerous, we are already reacting to it, usually before we know it.

Real danger—that's a crisis. Danger we project into a possible future—that's not a crisis, not yet anyway. That's a problem. And the two are very, very different.

WHAT **ARE** WE RUNNING FROM?

The key is to be able to identify when we're doing problem thinking and when we're doing crisis thinking. Everything that anxiety generates in us, all the energy drain and fear and worry and loss of life and time, comes down to this one issue.

Everything we experience when we get anxious comes down to a two-step sequence: first we conjecture/picture something bad happening to us, and then we experience the responses of Flight or Fight.

At the heart of this model is a very simple premise: we have two choices when we are presented with thinking that unnerves, worries or even frightens us. The choice we make either makes us anxious or puts us in position to stay calm and be a lucid problem-solver. We have to learn to identify when we are taking an issue and converting it into a crisis instead of responding to it as a problem. Just this single skill alone can do enormous good in our battle with fear and anxiety.

There are a couple of challenges to getting hold of this when it comes to fear work. One challenge is most of us don't really understand how much thinking we're doing when we're not aware of it. You might call it unconscious thinking. A better term would be out-of-our-awareness thinking—not so much unconscious (you're awake right now, right?) but whether or not you're focusing your attention on that particular thinking.

....

Just because YOU are not aware of thinking **doesn't mean you're not thinking.**

....

Think about all the things that happen in your body when you get anxious, but which you didn't consciously direct to have happen. They just happened, right? All those funky Flight or Fight responses could only start from signals from your brain—i.e., thinking.

A second thing to grasp about thinking and consciousness is the vast majority of us did not deliberately sit down and plan out what kind of thoughts we'd cultivate in our brains. Nope, we just *think*, in much the same way I used to eat potato chips when I was watching TV. Thank goodness I started thinking about that.

We are home to a host of assumptions, beliefs, attitudes, expectations, rules, processes and routines that run their merry way in our minds all the time—all without our giving them more than a moment's glance, if we notice them at all. That has huge implications for fear and anxiety.

For example, I don't like lentils. My mom used to make this lentil soup that was, for me, a great deal like eating brown paste. My mom was a brilliant cook, but I just didn't like her lentil soup. So by the time I reached adulthood, even the mention of lentils was enough to turn my stomach. All my Indian-food-eating friends told me I was missing out by not trying other ways to eat lentils, but I didn't have the time of day for them about the stuff. My reaction was automatic and immediate: no lentils for me, thank you.

Then one afternoon a buddy and I were having lunch at a little place near my house, and they had a soup that had leeks in it, and I love leeks. What I didn't know, and wasn't on the menu, was that it also had lentils in it. I slurped up that soup like there was no tomorrow, and only when I finished did my friend, with a smirk on his face, tell me that I had just eaten lentils.

THE LENTIL REACTION

Two things happened: 1) I found myself starting to get an upset stomach, and 2) I said to myself (thanks to this work on thinking), "Wait a minute. That soup tasted great. The lentils are not suddenly attacking my intestinal walls or anything. I was just fine a minute ago. Maybe lentils aren't so bad?"

And within a minute my stomach upset had eased, and I found myself shaking my head at both myself and the power of thoughts in general. I'm still sure I don't like my mom's lentil soup, but now I'm not at all sure that lentils in and of themselves are bad. In fact, I'm sure they can be pretty tasty under the right conditions.

What does that say about both the unconsciousness and the strength of our thinking when it comes to fear and anxiety? We have two issues around thinking when we go to tackle our fears—understanding that we don't have much practice thinking about our thinking (as opposed to just running on automatic), and being clear just how much that thinking can govern our bodies and our emotions.

THINKING VS. REACTING—PROBLEM VS. CRISIS

We do not have to be the prisoners of our largely out-of-awareness, problem-to-crisis thinking. It's time to stop the insanity. It is one thing to talk about turning a problem into a crisis. What does that look like in real life? What are some examples we can hang our hats on? It may not be immediately apparent to many of us where precisely we do this, or the subtle way this starts us down the rabbit-hole of chronic anxiety. By the very nature of anxiety, consciousness is not something we routinely bring to our specific fears/worries.

Since it is so essential to this fear-busting work, I'll say it again: a problem and a crisis are not the same thing. We blur the distinction in our thinking and in our actions, but they are very different creatures.

Problem: an issue, challenge, or situation that needs to be resolved, according to you. It is something up in the future, not for the most part in the present moment, and it can't usually just be solved by a quick fix. It requires some thinking, some planning, some work and some time. It may be urgent, semi-urgent, or just a good idea, depending on the distance from the issue in time and its importance to you.

Example: you realize one morning that you have a tire on your car that's looking low on air. The car can still be driven, the rims are still above the pavement, and you can probably keep driving on this tire for a week or more. It may not be the best decision, but you could. You need to adjust your schedule, hit a gas station or auto shop and get some air in the tire. That will take a little thinking and planning.

It is NOT a crisis. Nothing horrible will happen if you decide to wait until this evening to put air in your tire, or probably even if you wait until the weekend. It could evolve into a crisis if you don't eventually put air in your tire, but it definitely isn't a crisis yet.

Crisis: a direct, physical risk to your body and personal safety. If you don't do something right now something bad will likely happen. You'll get injured or even risk being killed. Action is required this second to either evade/avoid the danger, or to take the danger head-on in hopes of taking it down.

Example: you are upstairs taking a shower one evening and suddenly you hear a loud rumbling in the distance, and then your house begins to shake. You realize you're in an earthquake! Holy crap! You have to get out of that house now! You explode out of the shower and downstairs, praying everything holds together until you get out the front door. As you reach the door the earthquake stops, you see your neighbors across the street running from their house, and you realize you didn't bring your towel with you when you left the shower.

OK, I hope you never have that happen to you, but it did happen to me. Thank heaven I didn't run outside. And while I wouldn't have had a crisis if I had run outside naked (and it made a hell of a lot more sense to run outside naked than to run back for a towel and potentially get killed by a collapsing house), I would have been really embarrassed. The bottom line: I needed to act now to avert the risk of injury or death. It wasn't something to calmly contemplate, and there was no strategy to outline—I needed to get MOVING.

WHEN WE TURN A PROBLEM INTO A CRISIS

Let's go back to that low tire scenario. I notice my tire is low and suddenly I find myself anxious. What if the tire fails on the highway? What if I lose control of the car and it spirals out of control and I crash? What if I'm late for work? What if someone gets mad at me? What if my friends laugh at me for not checking my tires more frequently? What if I have to spend $200 on a new tire?

Well, you get the picture. Realize that I haven't changed any information from the original example. This situation is still only a problem. Your rational mind has assessed that you have at least a week on this tire before it becomes dicey to drive without getting it fixed.

But now I'm caught up in crisis thinking. I've decided (not deliberately, but reflexively) to treat this problem as a crisis. Now I'm generating scary possible futures. And, of course, I'm getting a little short of breath, and I'm feeling trapped, and I'm getting mad, and I'm getting that dull ache in the back of my neck, and—Flight or Fight is firing up.

Stay here long enough and I'll convince myself that one or more of those scary futures is guaranteed to happen, and now I'm really caught in an anxiety thinking loop. Super. This is really helping me deal with the tire issue effectively.

Anyone who fights fear knows how strong thinking can be, how it can prevent us from doing something we really want to do, or make us do things we really don't want to do, all in the name of avoiding our fears. Most of us who wrestle with anxiety are not just fighting one scary scenario in our heads. We've talked ourselves into making a crisis on multiple fronts.

Let's see—we've discussed earthquakes, tires, lentils. What are some other possibilities?

WE HAVE A WIDE VARIETY OF CHOICES

Here are a series of questions to prompt your own thinking of where you might turn a problem into a crisis. It is key here to remember that none of these are crises in the Flight or Fight sense. None of them can eat your face off or destroy you immediately. These are problems, and will usually only get solved if they are treated as problems.

Partners/Spouses/Significant Others: What if I make them upset? What if I disappoint them? What if they don't like what I'm doing? What if they disapprove of what I'm doing, or even thinking of doing? What if I wind up alone/lose my partner?

Being Alone: On the other side of this coin—what if I never find anyone? What if I'm alone for the rest of my life? What if I can never have a family? What if I'm not pretty/handsome/thin/ tall, etc., enough for someone else to find me attractive?

Work: What if I lose my job? What if I piss off my boss? What if a co-worker doesn't like me? What if a client/vendor/customer gets mad at me? What if I make a mistake? What if I make a big mistake? What if I can't find another job/what if this is the only job anyone will ever hire me for? What if I'm too old to get another job? What if I'm too young/too inexperienced to get another job? What if I never have interesting work?

Money: What if I run out of money? (See work above.) What if I can't support myself? What if I wind up on the streets/home-less/trapped? (See partners/etc. above.) What if I have to live on welfare or the support of family and friends? What if I can never buy a house/nicer car/go on vacation someplace exotic? What if I can't afford to buy classy clothes? What if I'm just not cool enough, if I don't have the money to buy/have/own this or that?

Success: What if I never reach my career goals? What if I'm stuck in a job I hate? (See work above.) What if my friends see me as a failure? What if I see myself as a failure? What if I never get that degree in school? What if I fail the expectations of my parents/significant other/co-workers/total strangers?

Don't think of this is an exhaustive list. These are just the big-gies. We can take just about anything and convert it into a crisis in our thinking. As you may know, there are people who are terrified of clowns, snakes, bunny rabbits and anything else you can imagine.

> Perhaps the hardest part of developing this first skill is getting comfortable with the notion that fear-busting requires some conscious, deliberate examination of our beliefs and assumptions. It means figuring out where in your thinking you've taken some issue, something we might even call a problem, and converted it into a crisis.

There are some easy clues, thankfully. When you think about something and you get anxious, well, you're on the right track. Another idea is to examine what you avoid, what you stay away from in conversation or in your behavior. There might very well be an anxiety-generating issue for you lurking out there. Remember my story about my avoiding lentils? What lentils are YOU avoiding?

That takes practice and some time, and this is essential for what I call unpacking our fearful thinking. Most of us don't have much practice thinking about thinking. That's not a personal failing: it is just that most of us have never been taught or trained to do it.

And this entire book has in a sense one purpose—to get us to that place where we CAN do some of that unpacking by looking deliberately at our crisis thinking.

TOOLS TO DO THIS WORK

So there's skill one: realizing that we're converting problems to crises in our thinking. Way too much of that thinking isn't happening consciously, and you don't have to be conscious of a thought for it to scare you.

You may already be crystal clear about what your fears are, or you may need to do some self-discussion and sort out what is making you anxious/afraid/constantly worried. Perhaps the best first step to do this work is to start a journal. If you're anything like me, journaling might sound as interesting as watching paint dry. But in fact, journaling is a highly effective way to have some self-discussion about what you're thinking, and it's utterly essential as you move through this work, for a variety of reasons.

What does a journal effort look like? It is my experience that you'll want a few sections:

1) In the first several pages leave room to write your identified "what if?" fears—the things you're converting from problem to crisis. You'll also want some room here to record what's working well, such as the tools and practices that are, over time, getting you to stop treating problems as crises. You might also like to keep some favorite quotes, some useful reminders of moments when things came together, or simply anything that keeps your thinking clean.

You'll only add to these pages from your daily or mostly-daily journal-writing as you work through what your anxious thoughts are in some clear way. I encourage you to put this at the front of the journal for easy reference when you need to be reminded about where your thinking specifically goes off the rails into crisis thoughts.

You'll also want to identify here the specific physical and emotional Flight or Fight reactions you have when you're thinking anxiously, because you're doing "what if?" thinking about these reactions too, and it will require work to stop thinking about them that way. (More on this in Chapter 9.)

2) The bulk of the journal is your tracking, in some clean and usually summary way, the work you've done in the day on your efforts for the four skills articulated in this book. Some things to note as you record your efforts:

a) When you noticed you were anxious, and your efforts to identify the thinking that preceded that anxious reacting.

b) The specific "what if?" thoughts that you can identify in that effort (for potential recording in the front of your journal).

c) Your efforts at self-care through the day (we'll discuss this more in Chapters 11 and 12).

d) What seems to be working, over time, with practice, and what seems to be slower to help, or even not helping at all. (More about that in Chapter 10.)

e) What environmental variables help or hinder your work. Those could include (but are not limited to) family, friends, co-workers, locations, TV shows, habitual things you do to burn free time (or in fact any habit that you've either linked to anxious thinking or that seems associated with moments of anxiety reacting), stuff you read, radio (including talk radio), anything that seems to impact your anxious thinking and/or the work you're doing to get free of it.

f) The good stuff that happened in your day and that's present in your life. This may seem like an odd thing to put in an anxiety journal, but as you probably already understand, anxious living has a way of sucking the joy out of our lives. Those of us who fight anxiety and its child, depression, NEED to practice focusing on what is good, useful, productive, hopeful and worthy of celebrating in our lives.

This journal will be a record of your work, a reminder of the "what if?" thinking that you have to get unpacked and cleaned up, and a reminder of the tools that work best for you and the things you need to rethink, change, get rid of or do more of in your life.

All of this work can also force a certain clarity and linear flow into the chaos of our thinking. And it can be very informative as you develop any history at it—you can see the pattern of your thinking written out, objective and very separate from yourself.

ENLISTING OTHER PEOPLE

Another way to tackle this is to talk with friends and family, people you know well, and ask them for their help. It can be very illuminating and useful to enlist other people in your work to get out of the habits of anxious thinking. I will discuss this in more detail in Chapters 14 and 15, but here, briefly, they can help in the following ways in the work of identifying problem to crisis thinking:

1) They can listen to you when you are working to sort out that thinking, and help remind you that even though you feel like it's

a crisis, they're clear it isn't. It is one of the great truths of anxiety that my fears are my fears, and when exposed to other people, they can be seen more clearly for what they are: simply anxious thoughts rather than actual crises.

....

Many of us do this in a desperate effort to get some

comfort. Comfort is good, and welcome, but there is a

need for the friend or family member who is assisting

you to listen first, then simply remind you that this

isn't, however much it feels like it, an actual crisis.

....

2) This is NOT your friends or family telling you to "stop worrying" or "just buck up and be less anxious." Not only is this not useful, it also tends to shut down our efforts to get help, often when we most need it. More useful comments include encouragement and not dismissal, such as "You can do this work," and, "I know this feels hard, but you're strong enough to do it."

What this probably mandates, for most of the people who will help us, is helping them understand the fight you're in, that you're dealing with thinking. It's vulnerable work, intimate work emotionally and personally. It will feel risky. Do yourself some favors here. Be selective in who you discuss this with, but don't shut everyone out to avoid taking any risks. Anxiety work is some of the loneliest work I know, and that feeling alone can energetically feed our anxiety and depression. As much as you're able, don't do this work alone or in isolation.

3) They can also help in this specific skill-building by helping distract you. Other people have the potential to pull us out of ourselves, and can help us avoid the obsessive, ruminating "what if?" thinking that we can get pulled into when we do this problem-to-crisis identification work.

A WORD ABOUT INTERNET ANXIETY SUPPORT GROUPS

When I began this work back in 1995, there was no Internet, and I longed for other people to talk to about what I was working through. Through the CHAANGE Program I did find a person who had fought his way out, and his counsel and support were invaluable.

CHAANGE, however, was concerned about the potential for anxiety fighters to feed each other's anxious thinking. Over time I came to learn this was a very real risk to be concerned about. In these days of easy Internet access there are lots of groups for helping anxiety and depression fighters connect and support each other. That's brilliant and can be outstanding. However, it is important to be careful with such groups. There's an enormous amount of misinformation in the world, even now, about what anxiety is, what can be done about it and what anxiety can do to us physically. That can overwhelm us if we're not careful.

Another risk is the temptation to feed our anxiety by listening to and absorbing the fears of other anxiety fighters or even other people in general. The energy of Flight or Fight needs to focus on something, and it will pounce on things that even vaguely disturb us when we're fired up with worry.

4) Another person who might be helpful is a therapist. Therapists of various stripes, including MFT (Marriage and Family

Therapists), LCSW (Licensed Clinical Social Workers), clinical psychologists, and psychiatrists can all be exceptionally useful in confronting and staying in this work. I discuss this in more detail in Chapter 14.

QUICK AND DIRTY ANXIETY RELIEF TOOLS

Part of the challenge of beginning (and staying in) this work is just finding some relief from the surge and press of anxiety in our thinking and bodies. A number of people (Albert Ellis comes to mind first in his brilliant book *Feeling Better, Getting Better, Staying Better*) have listed tools to give us some room to think and to stand down a little. Here are some of those tools:

Deliberate/conscious breathing exercises. Simply take slow, deep breaths. There are a variety of ways to do this, but the core is disrupting the shallow, rapid breathing generated by Flight or Fight. One great advantage of this tool is that you can do it anywhere, sitting, standing or lying down.

Full-body conscious stretching. Think of cats or dogs and how they tend to stretch. This is often taught as starting in our toes and stretching our bodies a part at a time—legs, torso, arms, etc. Again, the only goal is to focus on tensing and then releasing the muscles, again disrupting the tension and tightness when Flight or Fight is ramping up.

Physical exercise. This isn't about having to run a marathon. This might be a 20- to 30-minute walk. It could be some time on an exercise or real bike, taking a yoga class or exercising with a DVD program. The mission here is to exercise long enough to elevate our heartbeat somewhat and even break a sweat. The effect this has on temporarily reducing our Flight or Fight reaction is nothing short of remarkable.

Distraction/Diversion. We are not obligated to, and it serves us mightily not to, obsess over our anxious thinking all the time! We can become really rusty at thinking about anything besides our anxious thinking. It's legal and necessary to think about other things, focus on other things. We are free to get lost in a book or movie, get caught up in a conversation with a friend about something other than our fears and troubles, do a puzzle, play a game or take the dog for a walk. This in some respects is a kind of self-care, the fourth skill of Fear Mastery and what I discuss in depth in Chapters 11 and 12.

Focused work. This is really a kind of distraction/diversion, but it centers on focusing hard on a project or task, such as washing all the windows in the house, cleaning out the storage shed, washing the car top to bottom, or drilling down into homework or language study or anything else that requires intense focus.

Please note that I'm not claiming any of these tools will necessarily come quickly or easily for all of us. Some may be easier than others initially. All are worth practicing and using, to give us some mental and emotional space and relief while we plow through this work.

WARNING: this will not amuse your Comfort Zone! You will get pushback. You've been telling yourself for decades that these thoughts are scary, and so you've erected a Comfort Zone wall in your head, created by Flight or Fight. It won't go without a fight. On the other hand, at this stage you're not really pulling down the walls yet. You just want to know where they are and what's behind them.

Actually wading in and confronting your fears long enough to see them as fearful thinking (and not dangerous monsters that will eat your face off) is essential to preparing to take on the next step in the work: learning to discount the reactions of your Flight or Fight response.

WE NEED TO RETHINK OUR THINKING

Reprogram is another great term for this discussion. The basic premise of this model of fear and anxiety is that the problem lies in our thinking. This runs counter to how it FEELS, but that's the origin of our embedded fears and worries, and that is where the effective work to unplug fear gets done.

This work means taking on your fears. In case you hadn't noticed, this can be a serious piece of work! We spend years, even decades, telling ourselves (and programming our Comfort Zones) that this or that problem-converted-to-crisis is just too scary or hard to face.

It is to be expected that when we make the decision, even flirt with that decision, that our Comfort Zones will flare up and make it clear that this isn't anything you want to do, ever. That's all right. It's just doing its job of trying to keep us safe. Flight or Fight runs deep in us. All it takes is for us to think a fearful thought (i.e., something we've told ourselves is scary or frightening) and we'll activate that response system to some degree.

When you start examining your problems-converted-to-crises, you're bound to make your Comfort Zone scratchy—and activate Flight or Fight. Expect it. Prepare for it. Use the tools for relaxing and powering down that I've described in this chapter.

Expect pushback from your Comfort Zone. Expect to be any-where from uncomfortable to really anxious.

> It is also necessary to allow this process to take a little time. You didn't embed these fears overnight, and (as I seem to repeat here on a regular basis) it will take time to sort out and unpack them.

One last thing to remember: because you'll be bumping up against your Comfort Zone, you'll suddenly find all kinds of reasons to delay or stall or avoid this work. The room will need dusting, the laundry really wants your attention, you could just watch a little TV and do this later, etc. You know the drill.

These are actually GOOD things to do, and are a kind of self-care. By all means, take care of yourself. Just remember that taking care of yourself, ultimately, in this context, means unpacking the problems you've converted to crises—and converting them back to problems (we'll discuss this in Chapter 10.)

Here's the great news: it isn't nearly as hard as our fears would have us believe. Don't take my word for that. In fact, don't take my word for ANY of this material: try it out for yourself and find out. The work itself will demonstrate what works.

CHAPTER 9

Seeing Through Flight or Fight

You can run, but you can't hide.
Emily Griffin

Most of us are ignorant of the role Flight or Fight plays in our battle with anxiety. When anxiety first shows up in some conscious way in our lives we are usually bowled over by the experience.

Not understanding that anxious, "what if?" thinking is what fuels the situation, and not knowing that everything we're feeling and experiencing physically is Flight or Fight responding to that thinking, we freak out.

Some of us become convinced there is something terribly wrong with our bodies. Others are certain they are going crazy. Either one of these assumptions can feed a whole new raft of "what if?" thoughts, which of course make us anxious, which further feeds the spiral. (See Chapter 5 for a more detailed discussion of these misunderstandings of why we're anxious.)

. . . .

And through it all we just want one thing—to not be so

damn scared. So we see doctors, we see therapists,

we take medications, we try a host of things to find

some relief. What most of us don't understand is that

we're taking on the wrong battle when we focus on

Flight or Fight instead of the thinking that is driving

those reactions in the first place.

. . . .

The mission of this chapter is to get you to see through the fire alarms of Flight or Fight—physical, emotional and mental—so you can start to discount the significance of those reactions. Yes, we feel terrified, anxious, scared to death. That doesn't mean that we are actually about to die.

That's not easy work, especially at the beginning. Flight or Fight is strong. It evolved to be strong, to get us moving in the face of real, physical danger. The problem, of course, is that we're not about to get killed or injured. We have thinking that is making some issue or challenge a crisis-level event, but it's all happening in our thinking.

In case you're flipping around in this book looking for answers NOW, but haven't read Chapter 2 and my discussion of the specific responses of Flight or Fight, let me encourage you to go back and read those now. Understanding those specific responses will be very helpful as you begin to do the questioning I'm asking you to do in this chapter.

As we begin to turn to and identify the "what if?" thinking that is scaring us in the first place, we will activate Flight or Fight, and it becomes essential that we see those reactions for what they are: misguided, misfiring alarms to a danger that exists only in our thinking. This isn't easy. It **feels** so strong, **feels** so real, that questioning it seems absurd, or even dangerous.

We have also developed, over time, quite a habit of routine anxious thinking. This has meant routine activation of Flight or Fight and, for many of us, years and decades of running away both from that thinking and those anxious reactions. Even thinking of doing this work can conjure up Flight or Fight responses.

So, for instance, if you refer back to the list of possible topics that I mentioned in Chapter 8 as sources for "what if?" thoughts, even considering a "what if?" can be enough to fire up Flight or Fight. It is my experience, both in my own work and in doing coaching work with other people, that this is often the single thing that stops people from leaning into this work long enough to get some real clarity and begin to break the cycle of anxiety in their lives.

Of course, very few of us are dealing with just one "what if?". We usually have a basket of them in our brains, and every one of them has the potential ability to activate Flight or Fight in us. This is another reason we need to develop a practice of seeing Flight or Fight as not dangerous, not something to run from. As we wade into this work and identify and begin to change our anxious thinking, for a while we are likely to experience more Flight or Fight reactions than we'd ever be willing to stand if we keep thinking of Flight or Fight reactions as dangerous, or proof that we are in danger.

Finally, as I mentioned earlier, Flight or Fight can itself become a source of "what if?" thinking for us. What if this starts and never stops? What if I can never feel better? What if this Erik clown is wrong and this is a brain tumor, or proof that I am going crazy? What if this means I'm doomed to be anxious for the rest of my life? And so on, and so on.

Here's a hint: every one of those fears is also simply thinking. That's not easy to believe when we're in the grip of the surge of anxious reacting our bodies are doing—but it's no less true.

We have to also start questioning that feeling of hopelessness that comes to those of us who fight anxiety, depression, panic attacks and fear. Just because we feel that way doesn't mean we're right. Just because we haven't succeeded so far doesn't mean we can't succeed in the future, and especially if we have effective tools to help us succeed.

Many of us have been fighting this fight with inadequate tools and bad information. Many of us have been struggling in the metaphorical dark, alone, afraid to tell anyone about our struggle. Or maybe we have told someone only to have our struggle treated as weakness, as silly or just not real.

And all of us are sick of feeling this scared, tired and trapped.

I battled anxiety for decades. I had come to be terrified of two physical sensations and one emotional reaction, all based in Flight or Fight. The physical reactions that scared the crap out of me were vertigo and hand/finger numbness. The emotional bogeyman in my anxiety reaction closet was a desperate and overwhelming feeling of sadness.

It felt like the world was honestly coming to an end, that there was no point to anything I was doing, and that things could only end in failure and disaster. It felt so real, so damn real. I was certain that my feelings and physical sensations reflected what was actually true, or was actually going to be true further down the road of my life. As a result, trying seemed stupid, a waste of time, pointless.

That doesn't even touch the energy drain I experienced every time these feelings and sensations took control of me—or, rather, whenever I let them take control of me. I didn't debate it, I didn't dispute it. It just was. That sense of massive sadness could derail me for days, even weeks sometimes.

It was SCARY. I was in full Flight or Fight, and that was screaming at me to run, to do anything but actually stay and look at what scared me and endure how I felt. What I really wish I had known then was that I was simply in the grip of Flight or Fight.

My feelings, my physical sensations, were all the direct result of my thinking, and what I was thinking was making me very anxious. I was afraid of so many things:

What if I never finish college? That will make me a failure, right?

What if I never find someone to care for me, and for me to care for? I'll be alone for the rest of my life, sad and an obvious social reject, right?

What if I never find work that's interesting or means anything to me? That means I'll be bored for the rest of my life, right? What if I'm bored for the rest of my life? What if my life has no real meaning? What if I never do anything to leave a mark or make a difference?

What if I never overcome my anxiety? What if I have to feel this way for the rest of my life?

That last one was a real zinger for me, and could leave me flattened. I would lie in bed, wondering why I was even alive.

What I wish someone could have said to me was, "These are only feelings and sensations, Erik, and they spring directly from you activating Flight or Fight with your thinking." They needed to say a second thing to me as well: "They don't carry any more meaning than the truth that you're thinking scary thoughts, fearful and anxious thoughts. That is all they mean. Period."

I don't know that I would have heard it immediately. I was so sure that these feelings had to mean something true and profound that I could have easily resisted understanding this at the start. But just having the idea would have had the potential to change things much earlier than they did.

Here, almost 22 years after starting my climb out of chronic anxiety and panic attacks, I still find myself marveling at my freedom when I think about this basic truth about emotions. Do I still get sad? You bet. Anxious? Absolutely. These are natural and useful emotions. But I no longer treat them as crises.

The freedom comes in knowing that my sadness didn't just drop in from out of the blue, and that my vertigo didn't imply that I was dying of a brain tumor. I understand that Flight or Fight has a host of things it is doing in my body, and with my feelings and mind, and there is nothing dangerous or unnatural about any of it.

No, my sadness comes from something I've thought. I'm not always conscious of the thought when it happens, and it's very important to understand that. But with some practice I've become pretty stinkin' good at quickly identifying the thought or thoughts that have suddenly turned my mood.

THE POWER OF YOUR MIND

What sensations or emotions leave you low, leave you cratered for hours or days? And what are the thoughts that are generating those feelings in the first place? Remember, I'm not saying that your feelings don't matter, or that you're attempting to be a drama queen, when you have what seems to be an odd or unusual physical sensation. That is not the case. Nope, those feelings and sensations are very real, and very powerful.

They have to be, if they're going to be effective motivators when you're faced with real, physical danger. They evolved to get you to do something—either run, or freeze, or fight if you absolutely had to—so you could get away from danger now.

That doesn't mean that those feelings have anything real to react to. They are simply the servants of your thinking. If you are afraid of something, then you are almost invariably going to activate Flight or Fight, and that will generate strong feelings.

....

Isn't the human brain amazing? Here's some great

news: the same brain that can make us so afraid has

the power to make us unafraid as well. You don't have

to stay the prisoner of your feelings or the physical

sensations of Flight or Fight.

....

What physical sensations rock your world? Here's a list you can use to identify the ones that tend to make you anything from uncomfortable to terrified:

Dry or "cotton" mouth

Sweating, mild to intense

Tingling or numbness in fingers, toes

Whole-body numbness/loss of sensation

Racing heart/heart skips beats

Shallow breathing/rapid breathing

Tightness in the chest/a sense it's hard to breathe

Blushing, either just face and neck, or over the whole body

Nausea, ranging from butterflies to cramping and vomiting

Difficulty swallowing, feeling like the throat is closing

What feelings scare you? Let's do another list:

Sadness

Anxiety (Yeah, it's a feeling)

Nervousness

Anger

Rage

Guilt

Embarrassment (more common than you might imagine, by
the way)

Despair

Crying (the body's way of dumping stress from the body)

Nervous laughter

Finally, there are specific psychological reactions in Flight or
Fight that we can learn to be afraid of:

Stuttering

Disorientation/confusion

Inability or diminished ability to focus

Persistent distraction

Inability to remember things—tasks, words, intentions

Disassociation, ranging from a mild to intense sense of detachment from your surroundings or your body

This is a good time to take an inventory. These sensations and feelings are powerful clues that one or more thought patterns you have is/are making you anxious. They can point like an arrow straight back to the thinking that causes them in the first place (with some practice and review).

This is a skill. It takes some practice for most of us to even consider facing down those feelings, let alone track backwards from them into the fears that generate those feelings in the first place. That's OK. That's the practice that will really, actually give you the strength to do this work and get free of all that worry and anxiety and endless chewing over your fears.

....

It takes time for most of us to learn to patiently "lean into" the work of mastering our fear and anxiety. It is crucial that we be patient with ourselves, and that we expect some pushback from the Comfort Zone. Rome really wasn't built in a day—and you probably won't conquer your fears in a day either.

....

That's OK too. That's why it's called skill-building. It takes time, effort, patience and work. And that's the whole point, right? We're working to convert these crises we've created back into problems.

SEE FLIGHT OR FIGHT FOR WHAT IT IS

Bottom line: question what your feelings tell you. Question your reactions to your body. Fear and anxiety can make you feel crazy, worried, even leave you feeling helpless—but question it. See what thinking lies behind it. And know that it is possible to shake free of fear and worry, and possible to unplug the thinking that generates those feelings in the first place.

In the meantime, take your time with this work and remember that you are ONLY experiencing Flight or Fight responses when your body scares you. It will take practice to get that into your thinking—but just this single weapon can be very, very useful in helping you keep your cool as you unpack your fears. It will be tiring, it will take energy, and it will be frustrating. I can guarantee all that! But with time and practice, it will also be effective.

Recommendations:

1) Do this work in small pieces. Confronting Flight or Fight is exhausting and this Rome really can't get built in a day. You'll often have your hands full just learning to be present for your anxious thinking while you're not running from Flight or Fight.

2) Get very clear on the reactions, physical and emotional, that scare you in particular. Treat them, also, as "what if?" thinking, and include these in your journal. You want to practice the thinking that such reactions are normal, not weird, and not indicative that your brain is about to explode. That will come with exposure and practice.

3) This is a great place to practice the tools outlined in Chapter 8: conscious deep breathing, stretching, distraction/diversion, focused work.

4) Be kind to yourself. You don't get points for being harsh, punishing or self-critical when it comes to this work. You've probably had enough of that to last a lifetime. Give yourself a mental and emotional break when you begin to hear a fiercely self-critical voice in your thinking about this work.

5) Expect "spasms" from your Comfort Zone as you push on it. It can be useful to see our safety boundaries, our Comfort Zone, as a muscle, and when we stress it with exercise—i.e., push on that boundary and face into our fears—we will make it sore. In doing this work, so many of us find the courage to push hard, then find ourselves "mysteriously" anxious hours or days later. What happened? What happened is that we challenged some of our most basic fears, and our safety boundaries pushed back. It's actually nothing mysterious at all, but something we want to anticipate in a useful way, and not make into yet another crisis.

6) Also, be aware that we can generate a lot of self-criticism in order to give up and NOT face down the stuff that scares us. Again, be kind to yourself. You'll learn this and get skillful at this only over time, with practice and many mistakes. There are no points here for perfection, only for effort and steady practice.

7) Sometimes we just need a good cry, a dish-breaking session (I advise shopping at the dollar store for those plates), or a good primal scream into a pillow or from a mountaintop. These are healthy ways to vent and feel those feelings of stress, anxiety and fear as you face down "what if?" thinking and the resulting Flight or Fight reactions. That's legal and I strongly encourage it.

....

Part of what gets in the way for many anxiety fighters

is the sense that we shouldn't feel our feelings, that

they will somehow run away from us or overwhelm

us. Nothing could be further from the truth.

....

If anything, we are in desperate need to get honest about how we feel and allow those feelings to move through us. That freedom helps us both access our anxious thinking and helps our bodies and brains purge the overload of stress chemicals we flood them with when we do anxious thinking.

THERE IS NO DANGER HERE

Anxious thinking kicks Flight or Fight into gear. Our mission in breaking anxiety's hold is to start with identifying where in our thinking we are generating our "what if?" frightening scenarios of the future, and at the same time begin to learn to not take our Flight or Fight reactions so seriously. We have to learn to see them for what they are—reactions to that thinking.

CHAPTER 10

Converting Crisis to Problem

Sometimes you don't realize your own strength until you come face-to-face with your greatest weakness.
Susan Gale

n this discussion of getting free of the grip of anxiety, I've discussed how the problem begins: we learn to treat X issue or Y concern, not as an issue or concern, but as a crisis.

This problem-to-crisis thinking we've fallen into scares us. That in turn activates Flight or Fight, which has only one mission: to get us OUT of crisis. Period. There are a couple of skills to learn after we become conscious of our tendency to convert problems to crises. The first skill is knowing our fear is in our thinking, and that we have, usually without intending to, converted a problem into a crisis. The second skill is learning to "discount" the feelings and physical sensations that Flight or Fight generates.

A huge number of us get very twisted up/freaked out by those feelings and sensations. It is a distinct skill to learn to deliberately not invest in those Flight or Fight reactions with fear, worry and even terror. We feel the fear in our bodies and emotions, but the fear starts in our thinking. Getting hold of just these two very basic principles is gigantic, highly useful to anyone who is dealing with anxiety and fear.

Let me repeat that: I have the strong suspicion that without these two skills, most of us are at risk of floundering for years, decades, even our whole lives, lost both in our fearful thinking and in our fear of the reactions in our bodies and emotions that our thinking generates.

OF MOTHS AND MEN (OR IN THIS CASE, WOMEN)

Armed with these two necessary tools we can do the next thing. We can convert that crisis, in our thinking, back into a problem. A problem isn't anything like a crisis, regardless of how we feel or think about it. All of us know the difference.

Try this one. I have a very close, and long-time friend who is super smart. This woman has serious intelligence. She is rational, cool-thinking, logical, practical. In the midst of the storm she is the rock, the one other people turn to when things are going to hell, and she is the calm voice, bringing order from chaos.

She is cool and calm—until she sees a moth. Really, a moth. Now I'm no big fan of insects (definitely not crazy about spiders, although they don't scare me anymore) but you have probably never seen a person go crazy like my friend does when she sees a moth.

Let me say now for the record that moths can't hurt you. The worst thing they can do is land on you and flap their wings gently. There are no poisonous moths, and they don't transmit deadly diseases. I'm pretty sure we are way more dangerous to them than they are to us. But none of that matters to my friend. Normally the very soul of logic and sweet reason, she is instead reduced to screaming and shouting when she sees a moth in the house—or on the front porch screen, or really anyplace.

Why tell you this story? Because she has taken a problem, and in her case, a pretty minor problem, her discomfort with moths, and converted it into a crisis. All that cool demeanor and calm vanishes in the face of her fear/terror.

DRUMROLL PLEASE

This may seem like a silly or trivial example, except that it is a perfect example of what happens when we convert a problem into a crisis. Whatever her reasons are for being afraid of moths she is taking something that cannot possibly hurt her this moment and treating it like a life-or-death situation. As a result, she is in the grip of Flight or Fight, causing a serious decay in her critical thinking skills as well as a flare-up of all the classic physical and emotional responses of Flight or Fight.

Now, I have heard her say she knows in her head (when there are no moths around, and it is purely hypothetical) that her fear doesn't make much sense. She knows she doesn't need to react the way she does. She has skill #1 down cold. She has identified that she has converted a problem into a crisis. What she hasn't done yet is to move to either #2 or #3. She still lets her feelings and physical reactions (in her case, racing heart/sweating all over, plus sheer panic) carry way too much significance, and she has yet to seriously convert this crisis back into a problem.

Part of the challenge, as I've discussed in earlier chapters, is that terror and fear and worry feel so real. It feels like we should be afraid. So we do the afraid thing. We wouldn't feel this way if it wasn't scary, right?

Wrong, and thank God for that. This is a great example of how these skills are a set; we need the collection to make it work well. It often isn't enough to mentally know that something shouldn't be considered a crisis; we have to actively practice "discounting" our feelings and physical responses as well.

TREATING A PROBLEM LIKE A PROBLEM TAKES PRACTICE

It takes a little practice to figure out where we're converting problems to crises, to identify how we're scaring ourselves with our feelings and physical responses, and to begin to see our fears as problems rather than crises.

One of the most interesting parts (for me) about this thinking around fear and anxiety is the amazing fact that we human beings can become afraid of just about anything. We can take just about any issue, any physical object, any experience we might have, and learn to see that thing as scary.

And most of us know this from our own experience. My mom was famous for her fear of snakes, even though she had rarely seen a live snake, and never a dangerous one. There are people who are afraid of clowns (you may be amazed by how many people find clowns scary), people who are frightened by tight or low spaces, are afraid of the dark, afraid of swimming pools, afraid of driving, and, well, you name it.

Some of them had a bad experience with that thing or issue. Some of them had an experience that made them anything from uncomfortable to terrified once, by that thing or issue. Others of us haven't, but we're still scared of it. We may have learned that fear from someone else's fear. We may have built a story around that event, situation or thing for a lot of reasons.

But in every case, without exception, it wasn't the experience that scared us—it was how we responded to that thing or experience in our thinking. And this is the very heart of the skill of converting the crisis we have made out of a problem, back into a problem.

PLANES, TRAINS AND AUTOMOBILES

It is no secret that a lot of people are afraid to fly. And the last thing I would ever want to do is dismiss their fears and anxiety. I get that it can be very frightening to think about flying on a plane. It can literally stop the show for a lot of us—make it seemingly impossible to travel like we want or need to, stop us from seeing people we love, limit our career opportunities, you name it.

That sucks, to be frank. And it begs a question: how does anyone learn to be afraid of flying? It isn't as if flying is similar to riding a bike, for instance. Most of us have ridden a bike when we were young, and most of us fell off that bike and suffered skinned knees, scraped elbows, and injured pride. But I would bet that no one reading this book has ever been through a plane crash! Seriously—that isn't one of those things most of us walk away from.

Yet we can become terrified of plane travel without ever having had an injury or accident on a plane. You already know where I'm going, don't you? It isn't the experience that carries the fear. It is the expectations of what might happen that scares us. In other words, it is in our thinking.

....

We become afraid of flying because of what we think might happen. And those predictions can really scare us. They don't have to actually happen to us to make them feel very real.

....

My mom experienced increasing discomfort, then fear, then finally flat-out terror at the thought of driving. She went from a woman who owned and drove a Triumph Spitfire (and man, she loved that car) to a woman who gave up driving altogether.

She didn't have some horrible accident, and she was never injured or hurt in a car. That didn't make any difference. She literally made herself so afraid of what might happen while driving that it was less frightening to give up driving completely, rather than face those fears any more.

INDEFINITE NEGATIVE FUTURES

We become afraid of what might happen. That "might" can be anywhere from somewhat likely to completely impossible, but the actual risk is rarely the issue. That it could happen at all is enough (if it frightens us) to activate Flight or Fight, and off we go.

And of course our bodies and brains are assuming that this potential bad thing, whatever it is, will result in catastrophe, and that catastrophe will go on forever. (Don't try to read logic or reason into this—Flight or Fight evolved way before sweet reason did, and reason doesn't figure very largely into our anxious responses.) This is why I call these hypothetical outcomes Indefinite Negative Futures.

You know the drill. You finally find the courage to ask out your good-looking co-worker, only to be told thanks, but no thanks. Afraid of a negative outcome to begin with and now injured and incredibly hurt by the rejection, you begin to tell yourself this will never work, nobody will go out with you, that this is too painful to ever experience again.

You've just done a bang-up job of building a simple, individual rejection of the request for a date (which doesn't, by the way, in-validate you as a person or signal that you're Quasimodo lurking in a bell tower someplace) and turned it into something terrible, horrible, and utterly necessary to avoid at all costs. You've gotten caught up in the future, one with an indefinite negative that will never be OK and never get better.

IDENTIFYING WHEN IT'S DANGEROUS—AND WHEN IT ISN'T

In this series of skills, we have to:

1) Learn to identify where we are turning issues/concerns/problems into crises in our thinking, and

2) Learn to discount and stop being afraid of the physical and emotional reactions of the Flight or Fight response when we do convert a problem to a crisis in our minds.

Then we need to 3) Convert that crisis in our thinking back into a problem/issue/concern.

In doing the first two skills we identify clearly what is scaring us, and we begin to teach ourselves that our fearful responses don't carry any real weight or significance—that regardless of how we *feel*, the truth is we are not in immediate danger, and so fear and anxiety are not serving us.

In this third skill, we are moving beyond identifying our fears and instead working to rewrite that crisis thinking into problem thinking. We are disconnecting from the urgency of the Flight or Fight reaction, and we are doing the hard and crucial work of cleaning up our thinking. It is our thinking that is scaring us, and it is lucid, useful thinking that will stop us from scaring ourselves.

MORE ABOUT PLANES

So how does this work? Let's take the fear of flying example. Let's cut to the heart of the matter: most of us who are fearful of flying are afraid the plane will crash. OK. That is a pretty scary thought. I love flying these days, but I can rattle my own cage when I begin to conjecture about what a crash might be like.

Here's the thing: the current best estimate of the number of airplane flights in the U.S. is 28,000. Every day! And worldwide the number approaches 87,000. Incredible. That's a lot of planes in the air. Now, think about it. How many planes actually have any kind of problem, let alone crash? And of that tiny, tiny number, how likely is it you will be on a plane that crashes?

We hear all the time that plane travel is safer than driving your car. Well, that's really true. Your chances of getting killed in a plane crash, according to The Economist, are less than 1 in 5,400,000. Note that you're more likely to get struck by lightning or attacked by a shark! As I said earlier, it isn't really about the plane actually crashing. It is our fear of the potential future—our creating scary scenarios in our thinking, and then activating Flight or Fight as a result—that rocks our world and makes us run away.

GETTING CLEAR ON OUR THINKING

We have to drag out of the shadows, and into our conscious thinking, what we are specifically scaring ourselves with in our thinking. Then we have to challenge that thinking. We will of course experience Flight or Fight responses as we do that, and we have to discredit and discount those responses—they are just the product of our scary thinking.

This is the very heart of this work in breaking the hold of anxiety, and it is also probably the hardest part of the work, especially at the beginning.

In addition, we won't just find ourselves looking at one fear. Looking at a particular fear will almost certainly bring up other fears, which will also rock our worlds. These experiences will make us very uncomfortable, will make us irritable and restless and edgy, will make our stomach hurt or our chest ache or our legs sore, or whatever other physical responses we have to our fear. It will scare us.

And guess what? That's great. I know, that sounds crazy. When this notion was floated to me in early 1995, less clearly but in the right direction, I rejected it outright. But this is where we begin to find our freedom from anxiety.

By doing this work we're taking our fears on, challenging the bogey-men we've let push us around for months or years or decades. Those fears won't go without a fight. We have been telling ourselves for a long time that this or that thing, event or situation is too terrible to face. But it is a fight that we can definitely win—and it doesn't have to take a long time to see that victory.

....

Remember, our fears don't have to be big, grand,

or even make sense to anyone else. Remember

the earlier reference to the fear of clowns? All that

matters is that an issue, problem or concern rattles

your cage enough to make you anxious. Thinking isn't

always logical, by any means.

....

It also isn't always an easy process to stay clear on what we've converted from a problem or challenge into a crisis, as we move through this work. Habit and Flight or Fight both can make this difficult, especially again when we're just getting started, but even at some points when we're well into the work.

It can also be very tempting to get lost in the, "Hey, this is really a crisis, it will be horrible, I can't stand it," thinking. We've been sliding down that slope in our thinking for a long time. We've created a strong and easy-to-fall-into habit of worrying about this particular issue. As I've already mentioned, addressing one fear usually calls out others, and they're all in our face, rattling us and encouraging us to run away rather than sit with this practice. So "bumping out" of that groove in our brains will take some practice and energy.

Note: when thinking about issues as problems, it's useful to remember that for most problems there are answers, in one form or another. "What will I do for a living, how will I make more money, how can I find someone to love?" These are the sort of problems we can seek solutions for in our lives.

There are, however, problems for which there are no solutions in this sense. "How do I avoid growing old?" or, "How can I avoid losing people I love sooner or later?" aren't problems we can solve in the traditional sense. These are problems we have to accept as part of living in the world.

In addition, these big, existential questions are not things we can usefully address through the lens of our Flight or Fight reactions. These are the big, questions that take some thought, calm and time to reach any conclusions about.

A good example of this is my friend Karen. She is in her early 40s, married, has four kids who are already grown and mostly gone from the house. She is doing pretty well financially, and she likes her work as a teacher.

When Karen started this overcoming-anxiety work, things were weird at work because of the economy. Her husband is a good guy, but like Karen, he worries a lot. She wasn't certain what needed to come next in her life, as her role of "mom" had faded and changed from the crazed pace of the previous 19 years. So here were her worries, as she listed them for me:

1) Afraid of being downsized out of her teaching job.

2) Afraid her husband would be downsized from his job.

3) Afraid they wouldn't have enough money in their retirement account.

4) Afraid she wouldn't have enough money to help her kids when they need it.

5) Afraid her life wasn't as fulfilling or happy as it could be, and that she was wasting her time.

That's a LOT of fear and anxiety. From my experience, this example is pretty typical of the number and type of fears that a lot of us are carrying around.

In reviewing the skills needed to successfully shake free of crippling fears, Karen has done good work on Skill #1. She's clearly identified her fears. And she has worked hard on Skill #2, she reports—she is clear that for her, nausea, blurred vision, jumbled thinking and a huge sense of embarrassment were the Flight or Fight responses that made her even more afraid. Nice work Karen! She reported that just knowing this much has made the monsters in her head less scary and much less mysterious.

What about Skill #3?

IT'S GETTING DARK IN HERE

When Karen goes to tackle one of her fears (say, the fear about losing her job), working to convert that back into what is simply a concern, well, guess what? Suddenly her Comfort Zone shouts at her, "Yeah, OK, maybe this is just a problem. But what if you and your husband both lose your jobs? Then what will you do? That really could be a crisis!" (You don't recognize that voice at all, do you?)

Of course Flight or Fight starts to power up to protect Karen from the dangers she's now imagining in her thinking, and now the future is looking pretty black. There they are, Karen and her husband, both out of work, finances dwindling, money feeling tighter and tighter, bills stacking up, maybe facing the possibility of losing their house.

....

WAIT A MINUTE! She was just sitting there,

minding her own business, trying to calmly unpack

one of her big fears, and the minute she starts that

work another fear demands her attention. Now she's

got two big fears yelling at her, and of course that's

cage-rattling.

....

Lots of us, way too many of us, get so rattled by the multiple voices of multiple fears that we back away in a cold sweat (metaphorically and literally), unwilling and nervous about having to face into those voices. But what has actually happened? Has the future gone black? Are Karen and her husband doomed to a life of poverty and homelessness? Of course not. In fact, nothing at all has actually happened, except that her thinking has jumped into that worry groove and she has fired up Flight or Fight.

Nothing was wrong with Karen in those anxious moments. Yes, the Indefinite Negative Futures she had envisioned scared the crap out of her. Yes, her body and emotions were definitely reacting to those fearful thoughts. And yes, her fears ganged up on her. But that's all that happened.

DEFANGING THE MONSTERS IN HER HEAD

So how does Karen practice Skill #3?

1) She needs to keep in mind the central understanding that ALL of her fears are problems, not crises, regardless of how they feel.

2) Given the idea that nothing in her fears can hurt or kill her this second, or even today, she has the time to tackle her fears individually. She can get one fear unpacked, or start to unpack one fear, and defer her worries/work on another fear for that afternoon, or tomorrow morning, or even next week.

a) So she's afraid of losing her job. OK, she decides to give herself 10 minutes after work one day to sit and unpack that fear. She looks at her specific fear—getting a pink slip one day in her mailbox at school—and then works to examine how likely that outcome is. It is hard at first, and will be for a while. Just the thought of her losing her job can take her breath away and create knots in her stomach.

b) Maybe she writes to herself (does the journal work I've mentioned in Chapter 8). Maybe she has a verbal conversation with herself. Maybe she calls a friend and they think it through together. Maybe she does all those things.

c) Her goal is to assess just how likely, really likely, losing her job actually is. In Karen's case it is very unlikely, even in the current economic situation in her school district. Just getting clear on that can help her. But let's say she might actually be in a position to lose her job in the next four to six months. Then she is facing a problem, not a crisis. And it makes sense for her to start thinking through next steps. She doesn't (and probably can't) solve it right this moment, the way her fears want her to do. That's OK. The more she gets calmed down, the more she examines this as a problem, the better able she'll be to find solutions that work, or at the very least to think through useful next steps on her way to a solution.

3) She has to patiently, steadily keep discounting the Flight or Fight reactions she experiences in her body and feelings. At the start this can be a full piece of work by itself! That's OK. We won't unpack and sort out our fearful thinking in one session.

One good metaphor is thinking of your fears as a tangle of power cords in the house or garage. At first glance it is a hopeless mess. But the way you sort it out is one knot at a time, yes?

4) Karen has to take this in stages. It is very tempting for those of us who do battle with anxiety and fear, to try and do this work in one massive push. It's not useful for most of us. That means

taking breaks, getting and keeping our energy up and taking care of ourselves.

5) Karen needs to practice, both in her thinking and out loud, refuting the scary shouting of her fears. That can be as simple as saying, "Hey, fears, I'm talking to you this afternoon. Nobody is going to die right now, so shut up." Or, "I know things are going to be OK for a while, so I don't need to let you idiots ruin my day. I'll talk to you later." This may feel silly, but it *will* be very, very useful.

This third skill, converting crisis thinking back to what it is (at most, problem thinking) completes the essential skills needed to break the worry habit, the storm of "what if?" thinking that troubles our mind. It's important to be clear here that this is demanding, often exhausting work. It will consume a lot of physical, mental and emotional energy.

One reason this will cost a lot of energy is this work will make us feel anxious. There's no way around it. This is the thing we've been avoiding all this time, for however long we've been running from anxiety.

This takes some practice, patience and willingness to be uncomfortable while we work on these skills. We need to stay with our fearful thinking long enough to make some headway in converting crisis thinking to problem thinking.

Something that is invisible to most anxiety fighters is just how much energy our anxious thinking and reacting take. This work won't really take any more energy per se, but it will be much more uncomfortable than running, hiding or flinching away from our anxious habits.

We will also experience something I call aftershocks. Confronting anxious thinking "stirs the mud" of our fears. Often we can't predict when fears will surface in our thinking again, without our bidding, which will require yet more energy and practice to get through. This is why there is a fourth essential skill to make this work successful.

CHAPTER 11

Self-Care Basics

Life is ten percent what happens to you and ninety percent how you respond to it.
Lou Holtz

The fourth skill is very simple—self-care. While it's simple, surprisingly it's not easy, and not something most of us do well these days. That's particularly true of people dealing with chronic anxiety.

One defining characteristic of those of us who wrestle with anxiety is a remarkable lack of self-care. We are so hard on ourselves. We don't work hard enough, we are not smart enough, or ambitious enough, or successful enough, or wealthy enough, or credentialed enough, or you name it. We must try harder, and harder, and harder.

In that mad race to be good enough we often neglect the most basic kinds of self-care. We push the boundaries of sleep (something that is already dicey with many of us who fight anxiety). We are careless or oblivious to eating decently, and no, I don't mean we have to squeeze every calorie or only eat organic. I mean something like preparing and eating regular meals with some thought for what's less or more useful in the way of what we eat.

Then there is the touchy issue of physical movement and exercise. Again, this isn't an argument for us to become gym rats or muscle gods. Too many of us are terribly inactive, when even some small amount of regular physical exertion, such as walking, riding a stationary bike or any other physical activity does wonders for the management and mitigation of anxiety.

And there's one more place we squeeze ourselves very, very hard. Nothing seems to ever happen fast enough when we're dealing with anxiety. We want the solutions to happen now, not later, not with time and work.

So the end result of all this self-demanding and make-it-happen-now thinking, in our all-but-manic striving to be somehow good enough, is a lack of real self-care. This skill is crucial in our work to unpack our fears and disconnect/unplug our fearful reactions to our Flight or Fight responses.

The cold hard truth is we run the risk of sabotaging our efforts to get free of the grip of anxiety if we won't learn the basic skill of self-care.

EMPHASIS ON THE "SELF" WORD

Our modern civilization has a hard time with the word "self." We can get pretty scratchy with words like selfish, self-love, self-respect, self-esteem. Sometimes those things sound good to us. More often these ideas sound like, well, self-indulgence.

Those of us who wrestle with anxiety set pretty high standards for ourselves. The vast majority of us are holding ourselves to impressive (read: superhuman) criteria for who we should be and what we should be able to do.

I'm pretty sure you know what I'm talking about. We believe we should be able to work a regular job (or, these days, a 50- or 60-hour a week job), raise a family, save a zillion dollars for retirement, hit the gym every day, stay in perfect and flawless contact with family and friends, keep our houses spic and span, never be angry, always be willing to help other people, remain unfailingly cheerful, always get eight hours sleep and never get impatient with anyone.

We know in our brains (somewhat) that we're setting crazy standards, but our guts tell us no, we have to meet all these expectations, all these standards, or we're failing. In our anxious thinking, that makes us bad people.

One of the most difficult experiences I have had since I began this work with anxiety and fear was a phone session with a brand new coaching client. She had reported by email that she was feeling very trapped and scared by her anxiety. She was staying with friends, didn't want to go home to her family, was very upset and sad that she had derailed (for the moment) her work as a creative artist, and wanted desperately to get some relief from her anxiety.

As we began talking it became very clear that she was dealing with incredibly high self-expectations. She resented her parents' expectations of her, but was terrified to imagine setting her own course in her life. She craved her freedom but also felt she had to get started on a family. She was already behind in her own timeline for "success" and was berating herself for that.

And, of course, like so many of us, she was deeply worried about what other people thought of her, and was certain most of them saw her as a failure. No wonder she was anxious! Yet when we began to pull apart her specific anxieties she told me repeatedly that her self-expectations and conflicting standards (parents, self, friends) were no big deal, and she should be able to meet all of them.

She was somehow a failure if she couldn't meet all the expectations she had of herself, as well as the expectations other people had of her. It should just be a matter of turning off the anxiety somehow—it couldn't be that all of her shoulds and musts and have-to-bes were the problem.

IT REALLY IS ALL ABOUT YOU

Here's the thing: we're human. We have a finite amount of energy, of capacity, of stamina. We need a certain amount of sleep, we need to change our focus now and again, we need to exert ourselves a little physically on a regular basis, we need to get some food in us, etc. The very best thinking and research these days makes it clear that we have only so much mental space for problem-solving, only so much energy to make decisions, deal with crises, manage our lives.

The bad part is that we act as if we are machines. We're somehow supposed to run 24 hours a day, 365 days a year. We are not very skillful at assessing what we can reasonably expect from ourselves, and we tend to run until we're exhausted and have no choice but to stop/crash for a while.

And that insane expectation is made worse by all the rules and shoulds and have-tos we're carrying around in our thinking. Those inflexible, relentless rules tend to be the foundation for anxious thinking. While we are dealing with that anxious thinking, we also have to learn to start taking care of ourselves, and to start treating ourselves as human.

But what does that mean? It means, obviously, challenging the problems (and expectations) we've turned into crises. That is encompassed in the first three skills discussed in this book. But it also, crucially, means taking some time to think through what self-care is about. For this discussion, it means that we need to be patient with ourselves, supporting ourselves as we work to sort out the problems our thinking has turned into crises.

Let's start with one simple premise: you have to take care of you. Nobody else can do it. Other folks can help you, but you have to take charge of your own self-care. We each have to take the care and feeding of ourselves seriously, and we have to put it first in our priorities.

That sounds crazy to some of us. That sounds selfish, and self-consumed, and even heartless. A great number of us have learned that truly good people put other people first, always. We've learned that truly successful people put work first, or ambition first, or accomplishment first, or whatever first.

But what's really crazy is the expectation that we can be successful and not take care of ourselves.

LET'S START SLOW

The goal of this book is to communicate the basic skills that can make us successful as anxiety-busters. One of the essential skills we need is the skill of self-care. For the vast majority of us this won't happen overnight. It will take time, practice, and steady effort.

And that means we can't just put our shoulder to the grindstone and get it all done in one massive effort. The likely result of that mono-focus will be to make ourselves more stressed and anxious, not less.

We need to do this work in steps. We need to plan a session of identifying what problems we're converting to crises, and practice "discounting" the Flight or Fight physical and emotional responses that rock our world. And then we need to take a break. Then we go at it again.

Stages. Practice. A piece at a time. That's one

essential component of self-care. We are learning a

set of skills, and skillsets take time and practice.

I know from my days of battling anxiety that this piece of news wasn't something I wanted to hear, but it is a bedrock truth in successfully shutting down chronic anxiety in our lives. We have to expect that this work will be a major energy drain, and that, in the beginning, even that drain can make us anxious.

We have such high expectations of ourselves! We are supposed to just figure stuff out instantly, master skills effortlessly, make it look easy. It sure looks like other people are able to do that, right? That's crap!

Perhaps worse than our expectations that we're supposed to figure it all out quickly and skillfully (even when we don't have much skill yet) is the reflexive self-abuse we shower on ourselves when we fail to get it right off the bat. We slam ourselves, yell at ourselves, get mad at ourselves, and then throw our hands up in the air and insist that we'll never figure this out.

One guy I've worked with is a pretty smart character—a common trait in those of us that do battle with anxiety, as I've mentioned earlier in this book. During the time I was writing the blog that formed the basis for this book he seriously studied that blog, as well as looked at other resources on anxiety. In our first couple of sessions he reported some good progress at identifying where he's driven into the future by his fears, where he's converted problems into crises.

Then on our third call he told me that he wasn't getting anywhere, that maybe he was different, that maybe he was doomed to fight anxiety for the rest of his life. I was a little surprised, so I asked him what had happened. After some more self-berating at how obviously he wasn't smart enough to get this work done he told me that he'd had a difficult day where:

1) He'd had to work 10 hours straight.

2) He was fighting a sinus infection.

3) He hadn't slept well the night before.

4) He had skipped lunch because he just didn't have time to eat that day.

Then, on top of all that, he sat down (before eating dinner) and attempted to do some anxiety work. He got frustrated when it wasn't working well, so he pushed harder, then got mad, then (weirdly enough) had a burst of anxiety. Why? Clearly he was failing! Clearly he wasn't good enough or smart enough or strong enough to do this work!

HEY BUDDY, YOU WANNA CUT YOURSELF SOME SLACK?

High standards, maybe? Superhuman expectations, possibly? Or maybe just not a lot of skill at self-care? Hey, it's legal. Most of us are pretty bad at this self-care thing. All that means is that we have to develop some skill.

One of the hallmarks of chronic anxiety is simple exhaustion—physical, mental, emotional. The spiral of exhaustion feeds on itself, since we're still driving ourselves to do better, do it faster, do it NOW.

> How many of us have run flat out until we've literally made ourselves sick? Then we crash for a couple of days, annoyed-to-furious that we're "losing this time" or "wasting time," and then we crawl from our sickbeds, determined to "start being productive" again.

It's time to stop the insanity. And what is the definition of insanity? Doing the same thing the same way over and over again, and expecting different results. That cliché might have been written just for people who wrestle with anxiety and depression.

We don't have to drive our lives like that. It's time to cut ourselves some slack, to develop a slightly slower rhythm, to listen to our bodies a little better, and figure out what works for us.

I CAN ALREADY HEAR THE HOWLS OF PROTEST

What does it mean to take care of yourself, just for you? It might be something as simple as slightly lowering your expectations of your day. (Don't think I don't understand just how much of a jump that is for some of us. Even thinking of reducing self-expectation can sound like a recipe for disaster for those who battle anxiety.)

But, maybe it's enough, for a few days, to just work and come home and eat rationally and limit the TV to 30 minutes, then take a hot bath and hit the bed. Maybe it's taking a walk at lunch. Maybe it's deciding to not visit your family this weekend, but instead keep that time for yourself.

Maybe it means you don't attempt the anxiety work after a long day, or that you take a nap when you get home, then try some anxiety work. Maybe it means doing some self-comfort, like having peanut butter and jelly sandwiches for dinner tonight and watching sappy movies. Maybe it means getting a massage or just yapping on the phone with an old friend.

....

Here's the bottom line: this anxiety work takes

ENERGY. You must have energy to use energy. Self-

care is a vital way of giving yourself that energy.

If you don't, how can you reasonably expect to be

successful with this work?

....

Let's review some basic issues around the self-care we need to do to make that happen. Let's focus on some self-caring centered around our bodies.

BREATHING

When we are in the midst of anxiety, or even if we're just skirting the edges of anticipatory anxiety (what if I have a panic attack? What if I mess up this meeting? What if I smell funny?), we tend to move toward more shallow, more rapid breathing.

One great, basic self-care thing to do is breathe. Or, to quote the song, "Breathe. Just breathe." Stop, for a moment, and attempt to take a deep, slow breath. That means a nice big inhale, pausing a moment, and then breathing out again. It should take three to four seconds for the whole effort. Pause, and do it again. And again. And again, if you'd like. You can't help but slow down when you do this. If you have a hard time initially taking a deep breath, work to not make it a crisis. You'll get there. You won't fail this test. Remember to breathe from your belly. That means stomach out on the inhale, stomach in on the exhale. We're not breathing from our chest here nearly so much as our stomach.

We can find it hard at the start to get a good deep breath. We've been anxious a long time, which often means our breathing has been shallow and fast for a long time. That's OK. You can't help but breathe, and we want to breathe deeply and slowly.

This automatically dials back your anxiety. Not forever, and it won't make the thinking go away, but it will slow and calm your body (and even your emotions somewhat). Don't take my word for it—give it a whirl. Take care of yourself.

STRETCHING

Animals all get this instinctively—and so do we. When you stretch, you relax muscles and unconsciously begin deeper breathing. You loosen up the tight spots, and your blood flow improves.

You want to practice taking care of yourself? Stretch. Head-to-toe standing up, or lying on the floor, or even just leaning back in your office chair. Stretching makes you slow down, and automatically helps you come back into the present moment. It's great stuff as a short-term antidote to anxiety.

When should you stretch? Whenever you like. It's often more useful, especially first thing in the morning or if you've been sitting motionless in a chair working on a computer or watching TV, to move around a bit first. A five-minute walk and then a stretch session might be one of the best ways we can practice self-care in a small burst, any time of day. Couple that with some thoughtful breathing and you've just done a brilliant, contained piece of self-care.

FOOD

Food gets a bad rap these days. We NEED food. Sure, way too many of us eat too much, and we often eat stuff that isn't really useful to us. But we need food. Anxiety burns energy. No energy, no living, no fighting anxiety effectively.

You want to practice taking care of yourself? Eat for energy, and eat with even a small amount of attention to semi-healthy food. It might be easier if there wasn't so much information and contrary advice about what to eat and not eat. Try these basics:

1) Don't go a long time without eating. That doesn't mean eating every 20 minutes. Having said that, it isn't the best thing in the world to skip meals, and more so when you need the energy to move through and unpack anxious thinking. We need consistent meals, with some thought to what we're eating: some carbs, some protein, some fat, some veggies, some water. This simple

form of self-care can make a enormous difference to our energy levels, and hence to being more effective anxiety fighters.

2) Keep sugar consumption down. Sugar highs and lows are not useful to you in this work. That doesn't mean zero sugar. It does mean some awareness of when you're medicating with sugar, or any other food. (I've described in Chapter 6 that lots of us use food to medicate our anxiety. As we learn to unpack our "what if?" thinking, we'll get better at not using food this way. In the meantime, we can begin to notice when we're using food to comfort ourselves, rather than for the energy we need to overcome anxious thinking.)

3) Reduce caffeine, at least while you're still learning to clean up "what if?" thinking. With enough intake, this stimulant can generate anxiety reactions in people who are not fighting anxiety or panic attacks. So many coffee drinks are so strongly loaded with caffeine that you're better served cutting back during this work.

4) Although this isn't food, staying clear of marijuana is also very helpful. Marijuana has a tendency to make us paranoid, at least in its usually consumed state (smoking it). Having said that, there is now at least one form of distilled marijuana that seems to have removed the element involved in making us paranoid, and that seems to have some usefulness in helping mitigate Flight or Fight reactions to our anxious thinking. This isn't anything I'm advocating at the moment, as I think more research is needed before this is clearly established.

I know that for some readers of this book, even talking about marijuana is uncomfortable. Some of us learned that it's a recreational drug and bad in and of itself. Others of us have used marijuana for a long time to medicate the worst effects of our anxious thinking. Please remember that I have one, simple focus in this book: to provide the best thinking and tools possible to help anxiety fighters break the hold of anxious thinking in their lives. Anything that slows down or even cripples that work is something I'm going to advise folks to stay away from. I myself have never used marijuana, but that doesn't mean that for some people the original form or the new distilled, anxiety-comforting version might not be useful. The bottom line is for you to determine for yourself what is actually working, and what is helpful in your work to get free of anxious thinking habits.

5) It also seems very useful to reduce or eliminate regular alcohol consumption during the course of this work. Again, I know some of us medicate with alcohol, and it is an obvious next step to shake free of that habit in any way we can. (I define "medicate with alcohol" as the abuse of alcohol, the running away from our fears with drinking.) A glass of wine, a beer now and again, of course these are all OK.

Be thinking consciously about these pieces of self-care. Self-care involves taking care of the basics, taking care of yourself. This is essential so you will have the capacity to do this overcoming-anxiety work well.

SLEEP

We live in strange times. There may not be anything more important for self-care and health than good, regular sleep. Yet as a culture we seem to hold sleep in contempt. We're convinced we have so much to do and we are so pressed for time that sleep is the first thing to suffer, and often the last thing we attend to.

You want to practice taking care of yourself? Get some sleep. While it isn't completely clear what happens to us when we're sleeping, several elements are understood. We refresh our neuro-transmitter receptors, those keys to healthy thinking and feeling management. We sort out information we've learned during the day into long-term memory. And we give our bodies a chance to reset and recharge at the cellular level.

Start powering down 30 minutes or so before bedtime. Take a hot bath. Read a book. Watch some comedy. Listen to quiet music. Think about what went well today, not what didn't go well. Stretch. Practice deep breathing. Racing through the day and crossing the finish line five minutes before bedtime isn't helping anyone.

Self-care means letting yourself recharge.

Take care of yourself.

PHYSICAL MOVEMENT

Notice how carefully I avoided the use of the word "exercise." Some of us like to get out and move. Some of us have a bad history with exercise. We feel clumsy or stupid, or we don't like how we look. I've been there and done that. But I also learned that we are a species that needs to be in motion some of the time.

Physical movement does a great deal for us. It energizes us, and does a host of things for our bodies. It also seems to really help us function more effectively, mentally and emotionally. When I was first overcoming panic attacks, one of useful pieces of advice my doctor gave me was to start exercising. Things seemed less gray after a few minutes of exercise—I was thinking better.

Perhaps best of all, I was pulled back into the present moment, out of my "what if?" thinking, and that was a huge help, even if it was sometimes temporary. In those days any break was good—mentally, physically, emotionally.

So what constitutes exercise, exactly? The classic definition is getting our heartbeat elevated somewhat (60 to 70 percent of our resting heartbeat, for most of us) for 20 minutes or more. **How** we do that will vary depending on our current level of fitness, our current weight and other factors.

Most exercise gurus suggest that if we haven't been moving, we start with some walking. Just a decent 20- to 25-minute walk can be very helpful in starting down the road of regular exercise.

It's good enough, getting started, just to break into a

light sweat and feel your heart speed up a little.

The bottom line is that movement is good for you as you work through anxiety. Walking, jogging, swimming, dancing, riding a bike, hiking, you name it. Be smart, work to avoid overdoing when you're starting out, and think in terms of self-care. The work of overcoming anxiety is largely about habits, habits of "what if?" thinking and also habits of action.

Exercise is one of the most useful habits we can acquire in the work of self-care. So many benefits derive from regular exercise. It is helpful both in giving us breathing room from the moment-to-moment press of anxiety and in contributing to a healthier, more capable work with anxious thinking. I can't over-state how much we need an exercise habit. Self-care means letting your body move. Take care of yourself.

TOOLS FOR YOUR TOOLBELT

We make the work much harder, even all but impossible, if we won't take the time to care of ourselves in basic ways. It is about breathing, stretching, good self-feeding, good sleep, physical movement, developing some healthy perspective on how much we can do in a day, seeing this work as incremental and done over time with regular effort. All of these basic tools can strongly aid your work in mastering anxiety.

Please remember that habit development takes time. I'm not advocating suddenly dropping all sugar from our diets, exercising two hours a day, practicing diligent unpacking every hour on the hour, etc. I'm about the steady, thoughtful and (as much as we can) patient development of habits that will fundamentally make us healthier, smarter masters over anxious thinking.

Please also note I've only given bare-bones advice in this chapter about the elements of self-care I've discussed here. You'll find enormous resources on the web for all these topics—breathing, stretching, food self-care, exercise, etc. Just keep in mind that you're starting slow and not attempting massive change all at once. Start with one, maybe two steps of self-care at a time. Slow and steady definitely wins this race.

One more thought before we move on to advanced self-care: expect anxiety to push back on our work to develop good self-care habits. Anxiety has no shame. All it knows is to get us into a dark hole and away from whatever we've learned to think of as dangerous, as a crisis, in our thinking and lives.

For a lot of us that includes self-care, strangely enough. Self-care is something we've learned to label as selfish, foolish, something that takes away from other people, is only for weak people, or whatever crap we've learned to think around this subject.

So if we take a break we're being lazy. Recognize that little voice? Or if we take time to exercise then we're neglecting our children, or our spouse, or our job, or we're being selfish somehow. Or if we allow ourselves to only achieve half of what our anxious thinking tells us we should achieve in a day then we're bad people, or the world will go to hell, or whatever our fears are yammering at us.

ALL of that comes from our Comfort Zones, carefully cultivated over years and decades, just trying to get us to safety. The good news is that, in doing this work, we will find a brand new freedom to shake free of that old, useless, even destructive way of approaching life.

Self-care isn't selfish. In some respects it is the kindest, most caring thing we can do, both for ourselves and for those around us.

Why? Because doing quality self-care will give us the energy, capacity and strength to get free of chronic "what if?" anxious thinking.

CHAPTER 12

Self-Care, Advanced

Self-love, my liege, is not so vile a sin as self-neglecting.

William Shakespeare

Boundaries. There's a word I literally never heard in my life until I reached college, at least if we're talking about setting personal boundaries.

I had no idea of how little this was allowed in my family, and I had no clue how important this skill would be in getting free of chronic anxiety. The word isn't something a lot of us are familiar with as a regular practice in our lives. Boundary-drawing is something too many people learn to equate with being selfish, or being cruel, or being way too dangerous a thing to do because it will mean the end of relationships that we really, really need to stay safe or to survive.

The irony of that last assumption is that relationships need a certain amount of boundary-drawing in order to be healthy and high-functioning. More about that later. My mission here is to talk about why both our fear of drawing healthy boundaries in our lives is so scary to us and how at the same time we're feeding our anxiety by not drawing the boundaries we need.

ABOUT BOUNDARIES AND BATHROOMS

Let me start with a weird and uncomfortable example from my own experience. In my family's house in Las Vegas we grew up with a very specific kind of a missing boundary: we were not allowed to lock our bathroom door. I thought this was standard. Didn't everyone leave the bathroom door unlocked?

This meant that anyone, at any time, could walk into the bathroom, regardless of who else was in there and whatever they were doing! It happened all the time in our house. The worst offender was our mom, who, I now suspect, was the reason the bathroom door couldn't be locked in our house in the first place. I learned that I had to constantly be on guard in the bathroom, doing bathroom things, because you never knew when someone was going to charge in the door in, well, mid-activity.

I think about it now as an adult and it makes me shake my head. I think about the lessons it taught me and my siblings about what was OK and not OK to do when it comes to asking for respect around our needs and wants (i.e., it wasn't OK to have something as simple as a bathroom door that could lock).

I think of how often we were embarrassed by one person or another walking in on our bathroom activities.

Perhaps the most striking lesson from this story is that we were too often naked (literally) without being asked by someone for permission to be seen naked. That's a powerful metaphor for all kinds of not drawing boundaries in our lives. We are constantly having people barge in our door, one way or another, without our permission, and making us crazy, allowing ourselves to be made vulnerable without people respecting our most basic rights.

We need to start, metaphorically and literally, deciding when we're going to "lock the bathroom door" and start deciding when it is and isn't OK for someone to see us naked.

YES, ERIK, THAT SOUNDS GREAT—BUT WHAT IF I MAKE SOMEONE MAD/UPSET/HURT?

One time at the Kieser House I was feeling a little rebellious. I was in early high school, and I was sick of people charging into the damn bathroom. So, this one time, I heard mom coming down the hall, and I simply blocked the bathroom door with my foot while I was shaving.

Yikes! She insisted that I open the door, demanding to know what I was doing. I shouted back that I was shaving and that I'd be out in a minute. She was pissed off! Of course, once I wasn't feeling so rebellious, this ramped up my anxiety. "Gee mom, I'm really sorry, I wasn't doing anything wrong, I hope you'll forgive me."

What? What exactly had I done wrong? But that was my training. If someone else wanted something, even something as unreasonable as walking into the bathroom I was using without knocking, then that had to be OK, or I'd be the bad guy.

Sound familiar? Did you also learn that what you wanted didn't matter if someone else wanted something different? Did you come to believe that it was selfish and wrong to put your needs and wants in any position but last when it came to living, working, and dealing with other people? And did/does that go double for the important people in your life?

....

This might not be as big a deal if we were all zebras or some other kind of herd animal, creatures that expected to be jostled and crowded, and to exist in a minimum of personal space. But we're not zebras. We're human, and humans have a real need for boundaries.

....

One of the outcomes of not having solid personal boundaries is anxiety. I'll bet that sounds familiar too.

BOUNDARIES AND TERRITORY

There is a real, important connection between functional, respectful personal boundaries, and what is called in the social sciences "personal territory." The notion is that each of us has physical, emotional and mental territory that we regard as ours. It belongs to us and is important to us.

The physical territory stuff is easy to understand. Don't drive my car unless you get permission from me first. Don't charge into the bathroom unless you knock (assuming there is no lock.) Don't eat the last of the cookies without asking first. (That's a big rule in my house.)

But that also means things like personal space (how close someone can be to you before it makes you uncomfortable) and when it is OK and not OK for someone to touch you. All these physical territory issues can make us feel comfortable/safe, or make us feel vulnerable and anxious.

Of course, it is difficult (read: impossible) to talk about physical territory without talking about the boundaries of that territory. By definition, boundaries must be enforced to some extent, or they have no meaning. So, if we're not comfortable or don't feel safe alerting people when they cross our boundaries (hey, buddy, you're standing pretty close—can you back up a foot or so?) then people will, as you know, breeze into your territory whenever they feel like doing so.

But it isn't really the physical boundaries I'm concerned with, although they are very important and must be considered. Just ask anyone who has dealt with sexual or physical abuse. It is the mental and emotional boundaries that are my focus here, all the ways we trample on our own boundaries because of the fears and worries that feed anxiety within us.

DON'T COME IN HERE—OH, OK, COME IN

Let's say we have a belief that says something like, "I must always be happy in front of other people" based on a "what if?"? fear like, "What if someone thinks less of me or doesn't like me because I'm not always cheerful?" Then let's say we are having a really crappy day but we think we have to go see family or friends that same day.

What do we do? Do we go as we are, dealing with our feelings, just being in the place we happen to be? Do we allow ourselves to be human? I don't mean we have to dump our feelings all over the place and work to make others miserable. I simply mean do we allow ourselves to actually have our feelings, respecting where we are as we sort ourselves out?

We don't do that with the "what if?" belief I mentioned above. Nope, we go, we struggle to put on a happy face, we let other people dump on US, we pretend to be in a good mood, and we give away time and energy we don't have, all because we're afraid to draw healthy boundaries for ourselves.

Those boundaries might be as simple as telling those friends and family, "You know what? I'm not in the best frame of mind today. I'm going to take a rain check on this visit and see you all later." Or it might be going anyway and not pretending. That doesn't have to mean you rain on everyone else's parade, but it might mean not pretending to be Susie Sunshine either, not if that's not you right now.

That's just one example of drawing boundaries. Another might be, "I can never say no to a request from another person" based on a "what if?" belief like, "What if someone rejects me because I say no?" or, "What if I'm a bad person if I ever say no?" So when people ask us for what we either don't want to give (remember, boundaries include the stuff we believe belongs to us) or can't give away right now, but we give it away anyway, then we trample our own boundaries by letting others walk across them.

Ugh! That's not useful to us! And notice how we permit people to walk across our boundaries **because we are anxious about enforcing those boundaries.**

GOOD FENCES REALLY DO MAKE GOOD NEIGHBORS

So what I'm really saying is to become a good self-care manager, we have to face our anxious thinking. People can blather to us all they want about how we need to respect ourselves and respect our personal boundaries, but we won't do a damn thing about this until we look for the fears and worries that drive us to let people cross those boundaries in the first place.

Various writers and thinkers have come up with different versions of what might be called a personal bill of rights. These are the rights we have as human beings to take care of ourselves in multiple ways that promote mental and emotional health. This list of rights might also be called a to-do list for healthy boundary-drawing in our lives.

Here's a small sample of those rights:

The right to set your own priorities and to choose your own opportunities.

The right to say no without feeling guilty.

The right to ask for what you want.

The right to take care of yourself, including limiting your care of other people.

Of course, all these rights presume you also need to respect that those around you have those rights as well, and there may be some negotiation involved in the setting of priorities, about the consequences of saying no, etc. But that, too, is part of healthy

boundaries and healthy living, and makes for much healthier relationships.

....

All these rights are essentially impossible to acquire

and maintain if we lack good boundary-drawing skills.

Not supporting our own rights as an adult, healthy

human is a prime source of anxiety in our lives, and

we need the capacity to draw healthy boundaries if

we're going to be healthy adults.

....

Speaking as a recovering Lack-of-Boundaries Guy, I can say it
has taken some work and time to create this in my life. But every single time I've exerted myself and drawn the boundary I've
needed, it has helped bring some remarkable qualities into my
work, self-care, thinking and relationships.

Qualities like a sense of personal space. Qualities like self-confidence as I practice gently but firmly saying yes to some things,
no to others, based on what I want as well as what might work
for other people. Qualities like unplugging anxious thinking before it can start taking root in my brain. So I came up with a
term and a goal for myself. I am striving to be boundaried but
unguarded (spell check does NOT like "boundaried"—and I'm
not certain it is a word—but hey, how often does a guy get to
invent a word anyway?).

Let me explain.

WHAT LIFE IS LIKE WHEN WE DON'T DRAW BOUNDARIES

I didn't learn great take-care-of-Erik skills when it came to my interactions with other people. I did learn early and hard that my needs, my feelings and my goals came second to just about everyone else around me. I learned to shut down the expression of my thinking and feelings unless it was "safe"—i.e., it wasn't going to upset or offend anyone. I learned to internalize my frustration, my hurt and even my anger. I learned that safety lay, at least for me, in going stealth about large parts of me, keeping them from view, in some respects even from myself.

What this created was a life where I didn't have any boundaries around issues like my time and how I spent it. People could hijack my schedule pretty much when they wanted, my feelings and what I did with them (other people could tell me how to feel, and how I should manage my feelings), or even my personal goals (other people could and did tell me what to do).

As a result, I walled portions of myself off, creating a person who essentially didn't have much in the way of personal boundaries, but who kept big pieces of himself shielded and guarded from the people in his life. I was unboundaried, but guarded.

What's wrong with all of that? Well, for one thing, it created a remarkable resentment in my life. I didn't like feeling as though I wasn't in control of my own life. If anyone could ask of me pretty much anything, anytime, then I was handing control over to them. Never mind that it was a choice I was making. I was too afraid to not let people trample through the house of my life (metaphorically), too afraid of their being upset, or my being labeled a bad guy, to draw any boundaries. But that didn't stop my sense of resentment. I resented the crap out of the people in my life that could ask of me whatever they wanted—time, energy, emotional support, etc.—but were more than happy (and apparently able) to say no to me when I asked. It wasn't fair!

....

The problem, of course, wasn't them. I was the

problem, because I was (and am) still the guy at the

wheel in my own life. This led to a significant

degree of dishonesty on my part, with myself

and with those same people.

....

"How are you feeling today Erik?" somebody might ask. I sure as hell wasn't going to tell them, not honestly. I got pretty good at the veiled answer. "Well, I'm OK," or "I guess I'm doing alright," hoping against hope they would break the code and make a real effort to find out about me.

But that wasn't the worst of it. My dishonesty with other people and where or how I was paled in comparison to my dishonesty with myself. I wasn't talking to me about me, and it created serious disconnection within myself. I couldn't even be straight with myself about how I felt, what I wanted, what was going on with me.

And in case it isn't clear, that's not the healthiest way to live. A great deal of therapy, in my opinion, comes down to the therapist helping the client simply get bone-honest with themselves. Self-honesty is critical to good mental health, and that includes being honest about the boundaries we need to live healthy lives.

Still another result was a sense that I couldn't and didn't trust other people in significant ways. That stemmed from the first two outcomes. It was a problem because I developed this ugly habit of testing other people to see if they were safe. Did they make a "real" effort to reach out to me? Did they really want to be my friend? Did they really care?

Of course they kept failing the test because they were not telepaths. They couldn't know what I was thinking or feeling unless I told them. And I wasn't telling them, so they got down-checked and were not trusted. Doesn't that sound healthy?

Perhaps the outcome I noticed the most some days was how angry I felt. I was carrying around a big ball of hurt and rage and was often unaware of it until someone added to that ball by preempting my plans, failing to pass my test of sufficient interest/care for Erik, or by dumping their crap on me without asking permission. Since anger is always a reaction to anxiety (see Chapter 5), my anger stemmed from my own fearful thinking.

WHICH TAKES ME BACK TO BOUNDARIES

When I began to break the spell of anxious thinking in my life I learned at the same time I was in desperate need of boundary-drawing skills. I don't think I have to tell you that I was terrified of this subject. All of my training and thinking told me I was a crazy person for even thinking about practicing this ability on another human being.

Like so many anxious thinkers, I was trapped in habitual patterns of thought. I was convinced, down below my conscious thinking, that saying no to anyone, telling anyone what I actually wanted, being straight with another person about how I felt, was a recipe for disaster. I was already running away in my head the moment my therapist said, "Hey Erik, you have some boundaries to draw."

At that time, in the spring and summer of 1995, I was in a pretty unhealthy relationship. I knew I had to get out of it, but writhed at the thought. It soon became clear that if I was serious about getting free of anxiety I had to address a primary source of my anxiety: all my "what if?" fears about disaster erupting from me simply saying what I wanted, saying no when I needed to and my insisting on privacy when I needed it.

I ended that relationship. I agonized over the call, and decided to call from work so I would have to make the call short. I dithered at the start and then finally blurted out that I was done. Holy crap! All of my fears came running into the room, screaming at me. The person I was breaking up with was screaming at me too. There was a lot of screaming for a little while in that humble office.

And guess what? Three things happened.

1) I got yelled at, called a terrible person, had the phone slammed down in my ear, and then it was done. Wow. It was scary for about 45 seconds. I sure had some anxiety when the phone went dead. And then it was over. Gee. I was still alive.

2) And even better, I felt better. I felt free of what I had already known was a crappy situation, and from this side of the effort it didn't seem nearly as hard as I was expecting. Sure, my heart was racing, I was sweaty head to toe, I was sure I was going to hell for actually telling someone what I needed, and risking having them think I was the most selfish person in the world ever. I

was, however, also already feeling like I had lifted 50 pounds off my head.

3) I felt guilty later, over and over again, but I also knew that I had made the right move. I had respected myself, treated myself as someone worthy of self-care and better treatment than I had been getting, and I had demonstrated to myself that I had the ability to draw necessary boundaries.

And guess what? The guilt subsided as I got further away from that unhealthy situation and saw it more and more clearly. What in blazes had I been thinking, to let myself be pinned in a situation like that? The answer was that I had terrible boundary-drawing skills, and was terrified of anyone being upset or hurt by me.

THERE WAS ONE MORE RESULT

I also found myself less guarded, just a small amount, because I had demonstrated to myself that I could draw a boundary and take care of myself. I was calmer, slightly more confident, and beginning to understand I was the guy who needed to take care of myself, and stop waiting for other people to do it.

I know that sounds scary. It feels scary. But it isn't a crisis. It's only another problem, and one we need to solve if we're going to break anxiety's hold in our life.

GOOD FENCES MAKE GOOD NEIGHBORS, REVISITED

One of the debilitating things about learning to be an anxious thinker is also learning that self-care is selfish, or cruel, or ungodly, or some other untrue thing. Let's make sure we're all clear on this: learning to draw healthy boundaries IS self-care. Good self-care can't really flourish in the absence of our ability to draw clear, self-respecting boundaries—where other people end and where we start.

One of the most common places people walk over our boundaries is the use (and abuse) of our personal time/support. Those people will ask for babysitting help, a long-suffering listening ear to stuff you've already heard, assistance with a project they want to get done, or company for them to an activity they don't want to do alone.

Here's the thing: their asking isn't the problem. The problem is our thinking we can't say no, thank you. They are actually allowed to ask all they want. We humans don't live in a vacuum. We live in a community, a culture, a city or neighborhood or town, and we both have the need and the right to ask.

But we also have both the need and the right to say no (when it doesn't work for us). It's OK to say, "I'm sorry, I'm not going to help you with that." I know that sounds a lot like, "I hate you and wish you were dead" to some of us. We learned deeply in our younger days that any "no" was risky, selfish, arrogant or mean.

It was certainly true with me. I can say (with a certain amount of embarrassment these days) that I couldn't tell anyone in my universe a simple, direct, "No, sorry, I'm not willing to do that."

So instead I made stuff up. That was one tool I used to avoid having to say no. I had to build some pretty elaborate stories.

You might know some of these tall tales. "I am already committed to helping someone else." Makes me sounds pretty great, yes? "I can't help you because someone else got to me first, and I just can't cancel on them to help you." "I don't feel well." Like anybody believed me, but I used it a lot. "There was a crisis at work and I had to take care of that." I wonder what my friends thought of the companies I worked for. Clearly they were in crisis a great deal of the time. And one of my tried and true favorites, "A friend of mine was in crisis and asked me to come over." Again, I come off sounding anything but selfish.

But wait, the story gets better. As I found the tools to get under my "what if?" thinking and challenge the assumptions that had been scaring me for two decades, I also began to realize I needed to start taking into account what I wanted.

This meant if I was really listening to myself then I had to also start respecting myself and my needs/wants. Guess what happened? I stalled, I found reasons to not say no, all the while getting more frustrated and more annoyed, both with myself and the people who were asking stuff of me.

Finally, driven by desperation, I started one day saying no. A friend really wanted me to help him move. I've done a lot of time as a semi-pro mover for my friends. Sometimes it was great fun and it was something I wanted to do, but sometimes it was the last thing I wanted to do. I did it anyway and then bitterly resented the person I was helping.

Heart in my hands, voice shaking, I said, "Uh, listen, I, uh, I don't have the time to give away right now. I'm sorry, but I'm not going to help you move." I waited for the upset, the shouting, the accusations of what a bad a person I was. What I got, however, was "Oh, OK. No worries. I'll find someone else." I felt like I had just been let off with a not-guilty plea after murdering someone.

It wasn't always that easy. People got upset with me too. And some of that was on me. After all, I had been the guy who always said yes. They had counted on me to be the Yes Man again. That didn't mean I had to oblige them.

I was in a real sense changing the rules on the people in my life. And that was more than OK. It was time for new rules, for how I managed my own time and energy. It was more than legal. It was vital to my health and the health of the relationships in my life. It took some practice. I wasn't great at it for a while. I some-times gave in to fear and said yes when I needed to say no. This is an art, way more than a science, and we can only get better if we're willing to practice.

IT ISN'T JUST ABOUT DOING OR NOT DOING

And of course boundaries are not just about what we do. Boundaries are also about what we think, what matters to us, what our opinions are, etc. These are also places that healthy boundaries help us maintain good self-care.

Liberal? That's OK. That's what you think. Conservative? That's OK. That's what you think. Don't like shrimp? Totally legal. Hate shrimp? (Man, I hate shrimp. It's like serving erasers for dinner.) It's legal to hate shrimp too. Want to be a professional Alpine skier? Knock yourself out. Want to build a childcare center, or be an art critic, or get a 20-hour-a-week job because the kids are gone and you want to make some cash? Go for it.

....

The challenge with this is that almost everyone in our

lives has their opinion about what you should think,

want, feel or believe. And while that's nice, it is

still up to you, dear reader, to make your own

evaluations, your own decisions about what you

think, want, feel or believe.

....

Here's some weird news: if what someone else thinks or feels or wants makes you upset, guess what? You're "what iffing" about their stuff, generating fears about the future in your thinking. Same thing is true about other people's reactions to you. Here's some more weird news: just because other people don't like what you think or believe or want or feel doesn't mean you shouldn't have those thoughts, beliefs or feelings.

I'm not saying that all thoughts, beliefs or feelings are equal. Far from it. The validity or accuracy of a thought or belief is very much something that can be weighed and measured and evaluated. But guess what? You still get to have it and you get to decide what to do about it. And as far as feelings are concerned, well, nobody gets to decide how you feel. That doesn't make all your (or my) feelings true or useful, but they are still things that belong to us, and we still get to have them.

Will people get upset with us for having thoughts, beliefs or feelings that are different from the ones they have? You already know the answer to that. Just look at Fox News, MSNBC or any of the daytime shows like "Maury" to see what happens when frightened people disagree. Not useful.

That doesn't mean we have an obligation to take anyone else's perspective. We can also choose to listen or not listen when they try to change our minds. Never listening probably isn't useful, all the time. On the other hand, you may decide that some people do need to get tuned out, at least for a long, long time. That's legal too.

....

Putting up fences and drawing healthy boundaries will

trouble some people in your life. But they'll get over it.

....

That might mean they move on to other folks who don't have healthy boundaries (adios, I say; better for them and for us if they make that choice). They will more likely say, "Hey, that's cool," once they get over the news that you're no longer a doormat.

YES, BUT IT'S SCARY TO SAY NO

Sure it is. We learned to think we were at risk for injury when we first learned that we shouldn't or couldn't say no. Lots and lots of people have trouble with boundaries, either enforcing their own, respecting other people's boundaries, or both.

Maybe we're afraid we'll wind up alone if we say no, sorry, not going to do or think the thing someone is asking of us. Maybe we're afraid we'll have to look after ourselves, take care of ourselves—and we're afraid we can't. Maybe we're still afraid, consciously or unconsciously, that we'll be hurt, beat up or otherwise threatened with harm if we say no (all of which, by the way, is "what if?" thinking). We're treating future fears as present realities, instead of treating them as something that could be a problem if it happens.

The real question is, what do we need to do to respect ourselves, take care of ourselves? If, God forbid, we're actually physically at risk, well, that's one thing, and we need to think through and take steps to get clear of that context. But even that is an example of boundary-drawing. Nobody has the right to physically abuse us, trap us, or control us.

And that's an interesting thing to extend to our personal boundaries. Because if we're not at risk for physical injury, then it's time we started drawing the boundaries that work for us.

Some of that will be a negotiation process. Sometimes, because of how we live, who we live with, or the obligations we have taken on, we may not always get to have the boundaries we'd like 100 percent of the time. That's OK too, because we're still in the driver's seat. And nobody says we can't go back to the negotiating table and reopen discussions.

WHAT TO DO ON THE WAY TO BEING
BOUNDARIED BUT UNGUARDED

1) Start small in your boundary-drawing practice. The first step is actually being honest with yourself about what you want. This is particularly challenging for anxiety fighters.

What do you want for dinner? What do you want to do with your evening? Where do you want to go on vacation? What kind of work really interests you? You won't get here overnight. For many of us this is an evolutionary process. We slowly get better as we wrestle with these questions, become honest with ourselves, and then practice letting others know where we stand and what we need and want.

2) Invite those you love and care about into this work with you. You might need to start small here too. Pick one friend, one neighbor, one family member, and practice with them. Pick a safe person, by all means. Do role-plays. Practice saying no. Practice asking for what you want. Practice negotiating what works for both of you. Practice not just caving in because they seem upset or you're experiencing massive discomfort at even the thought of drawing a boundary.

Such practice is what the therapists call behavioral rehearsal. It might feel silly at first, but it is interesting in what it can do in the way of building confidence and make practice a safer thing to do (mentally and emotionally). And those you practice with might also benefit from these practice sessions.

There is also room here to consider who is helping you in your growth toward health and freedom from anxiety, and who is not. Many anxiety fighters wind up being fiercely co-dependent. (See my reference to Melody Beattie's excellent book on boundaries, *Codependent No More*, in the book list at the back of this book for more about this subject.) You may very well find you need to create distance for a while with some people in your life, those folks who don't want you to have boundaries, your own opinion, your own wants and needs. That will also be uncomfortable, scary, even terrifying, and excellent practice.

3) We need to stop seeing ourselves as victims. Being unboundaried but guarded means that we can slide into making everyone else the problem—they don't respect me, they don't love me, they don't get me. Well, my brother or sister, they are

not the problem. We are. We have to take command of our own lives. Breaking free of anxiety demands it.

This also means, however, that we can start asking for help from those around us, with the practice sessions I mentioned above. We can slowly become more honest about who we are and what we need, and solicit the support and help of others. This, too, is part of creating healthy boundaries. (Chapter 15 goes into more detail about finding help in this work.)

4) Expect a certain amount of pushback in your world as you begin to draw boundaries and take care of yourself. Family, friendship and work networks tend to resist change. People will have reactions ranging from mild astonishment to outright anger at your daring to have an opinion, to want something they don't want, or to your saying no to their request.

That's OK. This is part of the learning curve and will, with bumps and bruises, be an important part of our skill acquisition for boundary-drawing. It might be helpful to remember that we are not the only people in our world who have anxiety whispering in our ear. When we turn to face our fears and treat them as problems instead of crises, we'll rattle some other folks' cages.

Everything in Chapter 11 and this chapter is essentially about learning to take care of ourselves in healthy ways, many of us for the first time in our adult lives. I say adult because little kids naturally take care of themselves—attempt to draw boundaries, and ask for what they want. Sadly, we had much of that trained out of our behavior.

We need it back.

Expect this work to make you uncomfortable. Expect to find yourself reverting to old behaviors rather than holding these new boundaries you want to hold. Don't be surprised if you find yourself mad, or frustrated, or just pissed off, and maybe not even being sure why in that moment. This is scratchy work, anxiety-creating in a good way, and hard work, for a while.

This is a skill you'll come to be very, very glad you have.

CHAPTER 13

It's Like Learning to Ride a Bike

Fall down seven times, get up eight.
Japanese Proverb

The good news is this: you can end the reign of anxiety in your life. Some of you are already seeing that, in what I've outlined here, both in having a framework for anxiety in general and in the tools we've discussed so far. The frustrating news is that it doesn't come in a pill, and it doesn't happen instantly.

Believe me, I understand how that sounds. Any time frame that doesn't have the word instantly in it can seem like too much time when we're fighting anxiety. It is in the very nature of the origin of our anxiety—i.e., treating problems like crises, and as a result firing up Flight or Fight—that makes any time frame longer than about five minutes seem like forever.

....

When we're in crisis mode, when we are treating the

issues in our lives as crises, then we want answers

right now. Flight or Fight is all about getting away

from danger. Not later, not next week, but right this

second.

....

And while we may know intellectually that we're not in physical danger, we are still responding to the urgency of Flight or Fight's pressure in our bodies and thinking, "I am looking for the answer to my anxiety NOW."

I am here to report there is no instant cure. I am reluctant to say those words because I know that, in the midst of my anxiety-fighting days, I would have heard them as the cue to experience more hopelessness. Permit me to explain why this is actually good news, with a story.

When I was eleven years old my parents bought me a bike for my birthday. I had stalled on learning to ride a bike, largely from a lack of self-confidence. You could get hurt riding those things, it seemed to me. But all my friends were already Lords of the

Open Road, enjoying mobility and a freedom that I envied, and so I finally broke down and asked for a bike.

It was a beauty, let me tell you. My older brother's girlfriend at the time had a dad who custom-built bikes, and my parents had him make one for me. It was a sweet ride, with an electric blue seat, sissy bar on the back, cool grips—and it was fast. (Hey, this was the early 70s, OK?) There was just one problem—I couldn't ride it.

So that summer, each day after dinner, my mom started taking me out front of the house and began teaching me. In the beginning I was pretty sure I'd never learn. My friends John and Robin made it look easy, but all I seemed to be able to do was fall over.

I wish I had pictures from that summer of bike-ride-learning. There's mom, running behind me, holding on to the back of the bike, and me teetering along, often with my buddy Robin riding along beside us, shouting encouragement and then shaking his head when I went down one more time.

It just seemed so damn hard! Think about it. You have to pedal forward, keeping your balance, watching for what's in front of you and around you, and somehow steer the thing too. Sounds pretty easy from this side of the story, but I kept trying for weeks and couldn't seem to make it work. I began to think there was something wrong with me. Surely it hadn't taken my friends this long?

Of course there were moments when it seemed to be working. I'd start to get it, then I'd grab the handlebars too hard or get distracted and fall over. Those glimpses almost made it worse. Almost there, then boom, I'm on the ground again.

And I spent more than a few days and nights telling my friends I'd never figure it out, that I must be dumb or missing some essential ability. I'd never learn to ride a bike. It would be awful, terrible; I would be marked a loser, people would laugh at me.

Then came an amazing night in August when we were out practicing again, my mom running down Algiers Road holding my bike, and suddenly I heard my friend Robin shout, "Hey, you're doing it!" I looked behind me and there was my mom, yards behind me, waving me on and yelling, "Keep going!"

And I did. I had gotten agile enough to command the small handful of skills I needed to ride a bike. I did a lot of riding that night.

A SMALL SET OF SKILLS

We who battle anxiety have a simple mission in front of us: we have to develop some agility at the handful of skills that make chronic anxiety a thing of the past.

I discuss those skills in depth in this book. In this chapter I want to drive the point home that it will take some time, some practice, some falling down (metaphorically—this work shouldn't cause bodily injury) before you start to get agile and figure out how to get that bike moving steadily and well.

We have to figure out just where we're turning problems into crises. That takes some practice and work. It usually isn't immediately clear where we're scaring ourselves in our thinking. And most of us have more than just one problem or worry—we often have multiple, anxious thoughts trying to freak us out.

We have to develop some comfort "discounting" those Flight or Fight responses we're triggering when we have those scary thoughts. That doesn't come overnight. We've spent years or decades learning to be afraid of our shallow breathing, our upset stomachs, our racing hearts, not to mention the emotions that come boiling up when we're fearful—nervousness, anxiety, sadness, hopelessness, anger.

> We must learn to translate those crises in our thinking back into problems—to reframe them correctly as issues to work on, decisions to make, thinking to do, but not life-or-death, this-will-kill-me-if-I-don't-escape-this-now crises.

That takes practice, my brothers and sisters, practice over time, in the face of Flight or Fight attempting (and often succeeding, especially at the start) to scare us back into immobility and frightened inaction. We have become so used to seeing this or that problem as a disaster looming in our future that it takes real work to get it wrenched back into what it really is—a problem.

And through all of this we have to learn, maybe for the first time (or maybe just for the first time in a long time) to start taking care of ourselves, in all the ways I described in Chapters 11 and 12. Way too many of those self-care skills are themselves big challenges, energy-draining learning curves that at the beginning seem anywhere from impractical to impossible.

THIS IS A BIKE YOU CAN LEARN TO RIDE

None of this is complicated. None of it requires your mom to run along behind you, although the support of family, friends, spouses, a therapist you connect with and even total strangers on Facebook, can be very, very helpful. But the combination of skills takes time and practice and steady work. You won't do it perfectly at the start. You'll have very frustrating days and nights.

You'll get tired and mad and impatient. You'll tell yourself you'll never figure it out, that this won't work for you, there's something wrong with you, or there must be a quick fix someplace else. There are a lot of people shouting about anxiety. There are a lot of medications that seem to promise some form of relief, and it is so easy to make this all about just getting some relief.

It's normal to get impatient, frustrated, and angry with this work. Feelings of hopelessness, rage, grief and massive frustration will all be part of this journey. It's OK.

Just keep working, because you'll also start to see movement. You'll have moments of balance, then minutes, then maybe an hour. And suddenly, you'll realize you're starting to ride this bike.

You'll also experience progress, then have the sense that you've not learned anything at all. I call these moments "pop quizzes." We are given repeated opportunities to test our growing skills to manage problems as problems—and we don't always get it right. Problems vary in size, scope and scariness, and we will sometimes fall back into old ways of thinking and responding.

This is often magnified by being very tired (this work is tiring), overworked in the rest of our lives, or just not practicing good self-care. All of this is OK. Every "pop quiz" is a chance to learn again what we're learning—a little better, a little more thoroughly.

One last thing: you're not alone. There are a lot of us out here, and we're all learning to ride that bike. In the next chapter I'm going to advocate for finding professional help to strengthen your efforts and help you stay on track. Most of us will benefit enormously from that professional help.

Overcoming anxiety is learning a set of skills—skills that work together and create a new way of thinking about and reacting to the world. They are skills anyone can master, with time, practice and some (metaphorical) skinned knees.

CHAPTER 14

The Role of Therapy in Overcoming Anxiety

We think we listen, but very rarely do we listen with real understanding, true empathy. Yet listening, of this very special kind, is one of the most potent forces for change that I know.
Carl Rogers

Now that we have a solid understanding about what anxiety is and what we can do to break its hold on our thinking, let's talk about how we can get help and support to wage this fight successfully.

One of the primary sources of useful help is the assistance of a good therapist. While there are different types of therapists, the mission is simple: find someone you can communicate with effectively, who respects where you are, and who has some idea of the struggle and work you're facing in dealing with anxiety.

That sounds like it should be fairly straightforward. It isn't, however, so I'll spend a little time talking about the different kinds of therapists available to you, how you can decide more effectively how to choose among them, and what you can look for/listen for in your quest for a good therapist. First I'll discuss what therapy in general can do for us in overcoming anxiety.

WHAT CAN THERAPY DO FOR US?

The first great strength therapists can bring to our work with anxiety is that they can be great listeners. The good ones will sit with you and let you unburden your fears, and hold those fears with respect.

That may sound touchy-feely, but just this ability alone can be a tremendous gift. They can help you create a space where you are free to be completely honest, including with yourself. They can help you craft a situation where you can cry, be weak and sad and depressed and fearful, and NOT have to pretend that you feel anything else.

Too much of our time wrestling with anxious thinking is about how we look to other people, how strong or together or confident we think we should appear to the rest of the world. One of the frustrating characteristics of this condition is our tendency to create a front, an image that masks the actual battle we're in. A good therapeutic relationship needs to be one in which we are utterly free to be ourselves as we are in that moment, and free to be totally honest.

The second way therapy can assist us is sorting out where in our thinking we are converting a issue into a crisis, and help us figure out a more lucid, problem-centered approach for that issue. They can be great thinking coaches, and we need to be better thinkers around our fears.

Part of this comes from their detachment from us and our situation/world. Our problems are not their problems, and just that detachment helps them see our stuff as problems rather than crises. Part of this comes from the detachment they are trained to have as therapists—i.e., the professional boundaries they are schooled to have with their clients. Part of that detachment is this is what they DO. They help people sort out their thinking, as well as figure out ways to take action in the face of what concerns them.

A third gift of good therapy is having someone to help hold us accountable to ourselves for pushing ahead in the face of our fears. This is also really a coaching function, just like a football coach might do for his team. They can help us set milestones and encourage us even when the work gets hard, scary or overwhelming. They can gently push us when we're feeling like we'd rather just hide or delay in the work.

Anyone who has ever dealt with ongoing anxiety knows how tempting it is to run away, put this work off, delay another day or week or month. Anxiety by its nature leads us to head in the opposite direction from our fears. With a good therapist in our camp we have someone to hold ourselves accountable to, and that alone can be helpful and keep us moving.

A fourth capacity therapists have is they are not part of our family or friendship network. They are impartial but they are on our side, allies in the fight. Their mission is to help us, not make us conform to family rules or judge us for where we are failing or chastise us for not working hard enough. Their role is simply to help.

Our families and our friends mean well (for the most part!) when they try to help us with our anxiety. But counsel to "just get over it" or "it's only anxiety" isn't very helpful. Therapists are working for us, and that's a good way to see them—as hired consultants who have one mission: to assist us in breaking free of habitual anxious thinking.

To summarize, skillful therapists can do the following things: be great and respectful listeners, be skillful crisis-to-problem converters and coaches, be gentle and persistent encouragers in our work, and be independent but in-our-camp allies and expert consultants.

Therapy can be immensely helpful in our march toward freedom from anxiety, when we have a therapist who meets most, if not all, of the above requirements. There is, however, one more thing to take into account when shopping for a therapist: the quality of the personal connection you have with that therapist, and that is decided by you.

HOW DOES IT **FEEL**?

The best research at the moment concerning the effectiveness of care providers (medical and therapeutic, interestingly enough) says that the single most important factor in a successful relationship with doctor or therapist is simply this: does the client or patient feel good about that relationship? If yes, then chances are much improved for that client or patient getting where they need to go in their care.

That's pretty interesting, and not necessarily intuitive for most of us. It seems that many of us expect our doctors and our therapists to be cool, disinterested, distant care providers, and feel we shouldn't expect them to demonstrate warmth, interest or a sense of connection with us.

But that's exactly what this research says indicates the best chance for our success in working with our care providers. Some of this comes back, obviously, to the criteria I listed above in shopping for a therapist. Are they actually listening to you? Are they encouraging and supporting you in your work? Do you have the sense that they are on your side in this fight, or are just going through the motions of care with you?

There's another issue around the topic of professional care providers: we are often trained to accept that they are the experts and they know everything, while our only mission in treatment is to passively take orders and do what we're told. Even in modern medical practice this view is shifting (thankfully) as medicine learns that the patient is the center of the conversation, and what they think, feel and experience is at least as important to a successful diagnosis and treatment as the expertise of the attending doctor(s).

The doctor needs to be a partner, an expert advisor in the work with the patient. Their expertise is important, very important—but so is their ability to connect with us, to team with us to help us reach our goals, rather than to be the all-knowing professional who isn't interested in our experience, our journey or even our own personal wisdom and learning.

That's true for therapy as well! We rarely need someone who has no interest in or room for our input and experience. We need to run like hell from that sort of therapist. And again, we're back to listening as a crucial trait for any good therapist.

We need to go into our therapist search listening to our gut. Does this person feel good to us? Is there a connection for us? That doesn't mean the therapist has to be ooey-gooey all the time, or always hug us, or know all of our intimate secrets. Some people would run screaming from the room if that was the way their therapist dealt with them. This is about what works for you.

This is a personal experience, and different people will react to different therapists in more or less positive ways. The bottom line is YOU have to decide if there's a connection or not. If there is, and your first visit or two seems to demonstrate that this person has most of the qualities I've listed in this chapter, then you're more than likely working with someone who can effectively help you.

Some of us have learned strange or less-than-useful stories around engaging a therapist to help us, such as seeking out a therapist means we're weak, or lacking self-control, or other incorrect assumptions. But none of that is true. We see doctors if we have a bad flu or if we break a leg. Why wouldn't we see a therapist to help us with issues like anxiety?

It may help you to know that good research shows therapy (often in combination with medication) is the best way to face down and deal effectively with anxiety and depression. Let me quote directly from the American Psychological Association:

"While medication is appropriate in some instances, research shows that a combination of medication and psychotherapy is often most effective in treating depression and anxiety. It should also be noted that the effects produced by psychotherapy, including those for different age groups and across a spectrum of mental and physical health disorders, are often comparable to or better than the effects produced by drug treatments for the same disorders without the potential for harmful side effects that drugs often carry."

(www.apa.org/news/press/releases/2012/08/psychotherapy-effective.aspx)

A LITTLE MORE INFORMATION FOR YOUR QUEST

Most of us don't understand the general categories of therapists available to us. Those categories include:

Psychiatrist

Clinical Psychologist

Marriage & Family Therapist (MFT)

Licensed Clinical Social Worker (LCSW)

Licensed Professional Clinical Counselor (LPCC)

Licenses/training/skills will vary by state and country. More urban areas will often have a wider range of choices than do more rural settings. That doesn't mean that if you're not in a big city you can't find a therapist—you may just have to look a little harder.

Psychiatrists are medical doctors who have also done training in mental health. They are for the most part (besides regular doctors, obviously) the only folks who can prescribe medications (the exception being Clinical Psychologists, and those only in five states in the U.S.).

Clinical Psychologists are traditionally more focused on diagnosis and measurement/testing. They also, however, do therapeutic work with clients.

Marriage and Family Therapists (MFT) are all about relationship and family therapy—individual, couple, and group.

Licensed Clinical Social Workers (LCSW) are what the title says—social workers. They are professional service connectors for people in need of housing, healthcare, and other services. They can also do therapeutic work.

Licensed Professional Clinical Counselors (LPCC in California) are similar to MFTs, but are generally more focused specifically on individuals or groups. In some states they may also treat couples and families, depending on their training and certification.

Our search for a therapist ally in our work is much less about their professional credential than it is about the criteria I've listed for effective therapy in this chapter. I'm not saying their professional training doesn't matter. In theory that training should set them up for many or most of the qualities/skills outlined here. But that doesn't mean they are guaranteed to have those qualities and skills. You have to spend some time interviewing therapists and finding one who works for you. Empathy, good listening skills, a willingness to come to know you and develop a good working relationship with you, the ability to gently but firmly encourage you to do the hard work in front of you—these criteria are vital, more vital than a particular theory of therapy or a particular professional degree.

That might sound a little radical or controversial to you, and I can understand that. I, too, was raised in the thinking that professional caregivers have all the expertise, and my only mission was to passively accept that and follow their orders. Not true.

Why? Because if they can't be bothered to really listen to you, treat you as a peer and someone who has information they need to do their jobs effectively, then their help is going to be crippled to begin with. And if you don't feel comfortable or safe with them, you'll be second-guessing the counsel they give you and doubting yourself in the process, and you're not likely to be as honest with them.

Therapists have extensive training, knowledge and experience. They have important things to say and it makes sense to listen to them. But they need also to listen to US. And whether we're talking about physicians or therapists, perhaps the single most important thing they can do for us is listen to us first, and then offer counsel/advice/recommendations.

WHAT DOES THIS MEAN FOR YOU, THE CONSUMER?

You have a simple mission when you decide to seek therapy. You need to literally go shopping, identify two or three therapists you'd like to try, then go check them out. (Many therapists offer initial free phone or in-person consultations.) Sit with them, chat with them, and see what you think. You may even be able to do some of that over the phone and save a trip. Don't talk for just one minute though. Talk for several, and ask questions like:

How do you treat anxiety?

What is your personal experience with anxiety?

What is the role of medication in the treatment of anxiety, in your opinion?

Listen for their answers, and pay attention to how their answers resonate with you. Do you sense the potential for connection with this person? Do they listen to you, or talk over you when you're talking? Or even worse, do they talk down to you? Do you feel comfortable talking with this person?

This may mean having to decide not to see a particular therapist after meeting them, if you're not getting any sense of connection. That was hard for me given my personal anxiety issues, and this may feel hard for you to do too. That's OK. Do it anyway. You're not focused on making the therapist feel happy. This is about you finding the right ally in this work. Remember, they work for you.

For some of us therapy can seem challenging because we don't have a lot of money handy. On the other hand, it's amazing what we can find money for when we decide we need it. At the end of the day what matters is getting the help we need. Find the money. Often therapists will work on a sliding scale. Ask.

Going to therapy likely means leaving the house, which is harder if you're fighting agoraphobia (been there, did that). While some therapists these days will work over the phone or Skype—and by all means, find out if that option is available to you—your mission is still to get access to a therapist. If that means having to get out of the house, even while being fiercely uncomfortable, work to get out of the house for the little time it will take to visit a therapist. It's worth the sweat and fear.

If you're fighting a war, it only makes sense to get the best weapons you can, right? In the war with anxiety, one formidable weapon can be the help a good therapist can provide.

CHAPTER 15

Finding Support in the Work (Non-professional)

If you light a lamp for somebody, it will also brighten your path.
Buddha

One of the tedious aspects (one among many!) in our work to unplug our anxiety is the way it tends to drive us toward isolation, if we're not careful. It is disturbingly easy to retreat from the world when we fight anxiety and depression. This happens for many reasons, but for most it's a bad idea.

Our thinking becomes hindered, even badly hindered, by our anxious "what if?" thought habits. We are busy assuming the worst about lots of things. We are obsessed with how we feel. We are physically and emotionally drained. We have a hard time staying focused on where we should be in the work we need to do.

We are constantly tempted to give up, fall back, and get away from our anxious thoughts and Flight or Fight reactions. We are easily discouraged in these moments, and we can fall into sadness and a sense that nobody really understands or even cares about what we're having to fight.

This is where support becomes crucial. The Old Testament of the Bible states, "It is not good for Man to be alone," and that is doubly true when we are engaged in overcoming anxiety.

We NEED the help of other people to encourage us,

help keep our thinking clean, be there to listen to us,

and even push back on our fears from time to time.

So what does support look like? I think it takes two forms: 1) professional support (which I discussed in chapter 14) and 2) personal community support.

It seems to be a truism that those of us who make progress most effectively are the ones who can summon even a small amount of support from our personal circle. There are, however, several challenges we face when we seek that support, and there are things to keep in mind as we solicit and receive that support.

JUST TOUGH IT OUT!

The first challenge is the lack of understanding from the people in our lives about the anxiety we are dealing with. Like many personal problems it can be difficult (or even impossible) to "get it" if we ourselves haven't been through it. If you've never experienced a panic attack, or been seriously, deeply depressed, it can be hard to make a connection with how that feels.

Right alongside this challenge is a second issue—a common unwillingness to talk about these issues in the first place. Modern culture is frankly impatient with confessions of trouble on a personal front. Many of us have been taught to soldier on, tough it out, man up—you name the expression. It is often a sign of weakness if we admit we are anxious.

These two issues taken together can set up some stinky thinking. We feel (and fear) rejection from the people that we talk to because they don't really understand the struggle, and we're afraid that even asking for help means that we are "weak." Nobody wants to be seen as weak. It gets harder still when we do risk dropping our shields and tell someone close to us about the struggle we're facing, only to be met with bafflement or even rejection. Experience that once or twice, and it can seem nuts to try again.

We can experience this even with those closest to us, our husbands or wives, our significant others, our children, our closest friends. Ugh! The very people we need to be supportive and understanding are often the ones we feel we can't really make a connection with about this work.

WE'RE OFTEN OUR OWN WORST CRITICS

And if that weren't enough, there is a general tendency for those of us who battle anxiety to be very, very hard on ourselves. We feel like failures. We treat ourselves harshly, yell at ourselves, berate ourselves, and then feel even worse. We attempt to bury our feelings or hide from them.

So when others are dismissive or even just uncomprehending we can fall into the trap of thinking, "Yeah, what is my problem anyway? Maybe I am just weak, or lame, or flawed," or whatever we beat ourselves up with in our heads. Too often we have multiple hurdles in getting to the support that can be useful to us in this work.

SO WHAT TO DO?

We need to start with being direct, which is one of the toughest things for many of us who fight anxiety. We need to develop a modicum of comfort in asking for what we need and want. If we don't ask, it's going to be much harder to get the support that will help us. Along with that minimum of asking is the need to draw some basic boundaries for ourselves (see Chapter 12 for a more detailed discussion of boundary-drawing).

That's easier said than done for us anxiety fighters. One of the reasons we're wrestling with anxiety and worry in the first place is that we tend to internalize our fears, keeping them to ourselves instead of expressing them in useful ways. It means a fundamental shift in how we manage our feelings and our needs, and that takes practice.

Most of us know someone in our lives who seems to have no problem saying what they want. They seem to charge through life saying exactly what they think and feel, and also seem heedless of the consequences. They both infuriate us and at the same time incite admiration in us. We can do a little of that too. We don't have to be as "out there" and brash as these icons of self-care are, but we can certainly move in that direction.

It takes practice and time.

SO WHAT DO WE NEED FROM THOSE AROUND US?

Good question. I know I needed someone to listen to me—not for hours, but just for a few minutes, while I talked about my worries and fears and worked to think some of them through. It's amazing what simply being heard can do for us. When I say listening, I don't mean lots of advice or counsel from the listener. I mean simply being present and clearly paying attention.

Another thing I needed was simple support and encouragement, something along the lines of, "Hey, I don't have any idea what you're going through, but I care about you, and I'm here for you." It is amazing in retrospect how much I needed to hear that, how little I actually heard it, and how rarely I asked for it.

And it wasn't just words that I needed: I also needed someone to hold my hand (yes, even the guys need some touch now and then, and more so when we're in the depths of this whole anxiety/fear thing, whatever we're saying out loud). I needed someone to be around now and again, someone to hang out with me. I needed someone who was willing to just be in the room with me sometimes, even if we were not talking.

I also needed someone to get out of the dang house with me—to go on a walk with me, or take a drive with me, or even get something to eat, away from what often felt like the self-imposed prison of my apartment. Anxiety and depression tend to lead us to isolation, and that can suck the very soul from us and our days. Someone willing to drop by or walk over and help us crack the lid on that isolation is very useful in this work.

One thing that worked well for me leaves me in eternal debt to my friend Julia. In the midst of the toughest weeks and months of the work that summer of 1995, she made time three to four days a week to just walk with me at lunch along the Truckee River near where we worked. Many days I didn't want to go. I was suffering from the harassment of Flight or Fight almost hourly as I worked on my anxious thinking, I was tired and I just wanted to crawl into a hole. Her encouragement and patience was tremendously supportive.

One more thing that was useful to me from the people who matter in my life: they helped me distract myself from my obsessive "what if?" thinking. It doesn't need to be anything complex or expensive. It could be a DVD they think I'd like (and maybe popcorn too). It could be a drop-in-for-coffee-and-yak session. It could be just a phone call with the day's events or a funny story. All of these things are support for us as we work to unplug the anxiety that brings us down. And it is amazing how even a little of this can go a long way.

It's not really that complicated. It is, however, sometimes very challenging for us to articulate, let alone ask for what we need. But we need to ask for it.

Asking doesn't mean we're guaranteed to get what we're looking for. But we're a lot more likely to get what we need if we start asking. It doesn't make us selfish, which is what many of us find ourselves thinking when we ask, and it doesn't make us weak.

It doesn't make us anything except self-caring. Other people can't fix us, and we can't ask them to do that. We can ask them to help us and care for us, as we work to care for ourselves.

We need to also practice being patient when folks initially don't get it. Sometimes we won't get what we're asking for, or we'll get a debate about what we really need. That should come as no surprise to us. As I mentioned earlier in this chapter, if you haven't really made contact with anxiety directly then it can be hard, confusing or mysterious to understand what those of us who are dealing with anxiety are going through.

Because people often don't understand our work they can have a range of reactions. As I mentioned earlier, they will sometimes dismiss our fears and worries. Sometimes they will minimize them, and often from the best of intentions. After all, we're clearly unhappy and anxious, and it may seem useful to others to help us work to push aside or treat as trivial our feelings and thinking.

Sometimes those we love can get angry and frustrated with us. They want to help us. They don't really know how, and we're often not really telling them (or, if we are, we've tried once or twice and then given up) so they grow impatient or worried or both and dump it on us.

As I said, none of this is surprising. All of it has the potential to get resolved and more workable for us if we work to identify what we need. We need to tell those around us and stand our ground until we either establish that this particular person isn't in a position to help us effectively, for whatever reason, or we reach a functional understanding of what they can do with and for us.

GET THE SUPPORT YOU NEED

So let's start asking! It will be uncomfortable. We won't do it perfectly, and those who want to help us will need practice and time to give us the help we need. The number of potential people to help us will vary widely from person to person. Some of us don't have large families or friendship circles. Some of us have driven away the people who might want to help us, at least for the moment. Some of us will have to fight our fears of embarrassment and self-loathing for needing to ask for help in the first place.

That support however, can be a crucial force in helping us get to healthy habits of thought. So we can all start with what we actually have available to us, and then work to expand that circle of help.

We also live in a remarkable age of connection and communication. There are thousands of people online who are looking for the same kind of help you're seeking in this book, and which you may have in fact already begun tapping into. So regardless of our immediate potential support networks there are lots of people online who we can connect with and gather support from in our work.

A word of caution: look carefully at the support groups that are available, and vet the people you're going to be connected to before you get too involved. There is an enormous amount of misinformation on the web (and in the world in general) about anxiety and what can be done about it.

In addition, it is easy when we are fighting anxiety to feed off other people's anxiety as well. You will find people on the Internet who are getting a handle on their thinking and can be supportive without spraying their anxiety on you. You will find others who spray others all the time with their fear.

I'm not faulting them for that. We can get very desperate and scared when we are hip-deep in our "what if?" thinking. But it doesn't serve our own progress to get caught up in other folks' anxious thinking.

Finally, we have to remember the boundary work of Chapter 12 and stay clear on what we can and can't do for other people. In looking for help ourselves we can be drawn into giving away time and energy that we simply don't have to spare to other people. Support, encouragement, reminders of what's useful and the occasional shoulder to cry on are all very, very helpful. Spending hours listening to other people's fears or becoming someone else's "safe person" is not helpful and should be avoided at all costs. Finally, while online support can be wonderful and very helpful, I truly believe that we are often better served by people close at hand, and we want to bend some effort to gaining what we can get locally.

In the next chapter I'm going to spend a little time talking about the principal obstacles we run into as we do this work, what slows us down, and what we can do about those obstacles.

CHAPTER 16

Five Ways We Trip Ourselves Up in This Work

Success is not final, failure is not fatal. It is the courage to continue that counts.
Winston Churchill

I t would be great to think that we could just take the information in this book, apply it, practice for a little while and BAM—be free of anxiety.

Yet for most of us it isn't that easy. We didn't get our anxious thinking overnight, and we often don't give up the habits of anxious thinking as easily as we'd like.

As you read through the typical barriers to getting free from anxiety that I've listed in this chapter, let me encourage you to avoid using these as weapons of self-abuse. Anxiety is one of the most insidious mind games we can play with ourselves. By its very nature it is something that leads us away from the work to get free of it. Everyone who fights anxiety, and I mean everyone, is reluctant to wade into and keep wading into that work. It's uncomfortable, it's often scary, it's exhausting.

So please, cut yourself some slack if you see yourself in one or more of these pitfalls. You are always free to start climbing out again, but it's more useful if we're kind to ourselves, patient and even willing to make some mistakes now and again as we make our way.

1) CONTINUING TO RUN FROM FLIGHT OR FIGHT FEELINGS AND SENSATIONS

I have been doing anxiety coaching for a number of years, and I can say with a lot of confidence that the impulse to run is probably right up at the top of the list of the reasons people get stalled in this work. It is so easy to do. While not everyone who falls into the vortex of chronic anxiety winds up terrified of one or more Flight or Fight sensations or feelings, most of us do. We wind up letting those scary sensations and feelings increasingly wall us away from life and the world.

Because we're ramped up with anxiety we feel like we're in danger—and that's all Flight or Fight needs. But we're not being attacked. We're scaring ourselves in our thinking, and in so doing we're firing up Flight or Fight. We have to turn and face down those sensations. Too many of us, not understanding what was happening in the early days of our anxiety, scared ourselves silly with fearful reacting to the reactions of Flight or Fight—and we've been running scared ever since.

....

Without intending to, we've trained ourselves to think

those sensations and emotions are just too scary,

just too real-feeling to face down. So we get stuck, or

worse, keep retreating from the world, trying to get

away from how we feel.

....

When we do that, anxiety continues to rule our lives. We have to rethink our assumptions about Flight or Fight and how it affects us. We have to turn into the wind, metaphorically, and stay turned long enough to wade through our anxious reactions to Flight or Fight.

We are not in danger from what we feel, physically or emotionally. Sooner or later, if we want off of the anxiety merry-go-round, we have to face the tedious and frightening responses of Flight or Fight and see them for what they are—reactions, and nothing else.

It isn't enough to just endure Flight or Fight's storm in our bodies and emotions. At the same time, we have to challenge our thinking about it, identify where we have scared ourselves with those sensations and feelings, and change the story we have about those feelings and sensations. It takes time. It is damn uncomfortable to boot. But it is absolutely essential if we want to get clear of anxiety.

2) AVOIDING THE "UNPACKING" OF THE THINKING THAT MADE US ANXIOUS IN THE FIRST PLACE

Anxiety does not come out of nowhere. It invariably begins in our thinking. Those Flight or Fight sensations I mentioned above? They had to start with thinking that made us anxious first. There really is a chicken-and-egg sequence in this work.

Where are we turning issues in our lives into crises in our thinking? This is the heart of the work. We can do therapy; we can take medications that alleviate some or all of those Flight or Fight reactions; we can exercise, meditate, or work three jobs. But until we unpack our anxious thinking, nothing fundamentally will change about our anxiety.

This is usually an uncomfortable process. By definition, if we had been comfortable identifying and facing down the thinking that made us anxious, we likely wouldn't be fighting anxiety right now. Instead we ran away from that thinking (if we were even conscious of that thinking to begin with) and now we reflexively, unconsciously, flinch away if we even get close to it.

And of course, if we get close, Flight or Fight fires up. Ugh! We don't want to do this work! Make it all just go away! I've said that, and I've heard a lot of other people say it too.

The bad news is, it won't just go away. We have to identify it and change our crisis thinking to what it really needs to be: problem thinking. It's uncomfortable, even damn uncomfortable, but that doesn't change the need to do it.

The good news is that it is literally the lynchpin of all this anxiety that plagues us, and in doing this work we can break free, well and truly, from a life crippled by anxiety. It is a steady, often slow, often frustrating and scratchy process, but it is the way out.

3) INSISTING THAT SOMETHING IS PHYSICALLY WRONG WHEN WE HAVEN'T REALLY CHALLENGED OUR ANXIOUS THINKING

Many of us, desperate to find a way to get some relief from how scared and trapped we feel, search long and hard for some clear medical reason for our anxiety. It isn't a foolish thing to do. We are feeling in our bodies all these strange and terrifying sensations. Our bodies seem out of control. Real, physical things are rocking our worlds, disrupting our lives. It seems logical to find physical causes for these events.

The problem is that way too often, once we start this quest, we find ourselves back at the doctor's office or emergency room again and again and again. Usually we're just making ourselves more frustrated and anxious at what we find, which is nothing. We get our blood pressure checked, our hearts examined, blood samples taken, answer a battery of questions and then we get told there isn't anything wrong.

However, there isn't much comfort in being told nothing is wrong, because we're still having these physical things cascade through our bodies: heart racing, breath labored and shallow, nausea doubling us over, etc. There has to be something physically wrong, right?

No. Actually there doesn't have to be anything physically askew. This is Flight or Fight responding to our fearful thinking. That's big news for some of us. And that's hard news for some of us as well. It's hard sometimes because we really don't want to face down the thinking that scares us. And it's hard news because we can harbor a hope that some pill or some treatment will make all of this fear and worry STOP.

The problem isn't in how we feel.

It is in what we think.

I'm not saying that we shouldn't go see a doctor if we're having physical sensations or changes that scare us. By all means see the doctor. It is way, WAY better to have that examination and assessment, and the accompanying solid information it can provide us about our physical health, than it is to not know.

The mission isn't to avoid the doctor. The mission is, once we have that, "Hey, we can't find anything wrong with you physically," to get down to the work of sorting out our anxious thinking.

And, of course, there is a group of us that are both afraid to see the doctor and afraid of what's happening to us in our bodies—the proverbial rock and a hard place. Let's be clear: there's no rock or hard place. There's just anxious thinking that's got us boxed into the corner for the moment. All of that is about addressing the fearful thinking that is hobbling us.

Our fears want us to just sit down, not move and wait for the anxiety to go away. It isn't going to happen. Sooner or later we have to get up and make a move toward one or another Comfort Zone wall if we're going to break the hold of anxiety in our lives.

Here's another reason we can find ourselves not making progress in our work:

4) REFUSING TO ACCEPT DISCOMFORT AS PART OF THE JOURNEY

As anxiety fighters we learn way too early and too well to not be very kind to ourselves. We can engage very quickly in pretty self-abusive self-talk about how weak we are, how stupid we are, how much we suck, etc. So I address this next topic with some nervousness. Let me be clear: I am not accusing any of us of being weak or stupid. I am saying that it is very tempting to step back, and keep stepping back, from being uncomfortable. Uncomfortable is really a poor description. We step back from being scared out of our wits, at least at the start. Then at some point we keep flinching back from the memories of that fear whenever we get a twinge, an unexpected Flight or Fight sensation or a fearful thought.

And before you know it we're sitting in our house, afraid to go out or even to leave just one room of our house. We're avoiding even getting close to being uncomfortable for fear of waking the sleeping tiger of our fears. We hate being trapped and shut down, but we hate even more the notion that we're going to have to deal with that fear and our reactions to our fear again.

It is completely natural to flinch back from scary things. That kept our forebears alive in the face of some serious danger. But we're not in physical danger when we're fighting anxiety.

....

We have to begin the very uncomfortable but
absolutely necessary work of looking our fear in
the eye and learning that it can't hurt us, however
much it scares us.

....

We have to essentially get comfortable with some discomfort
on the way to our freedom. It's easy to say, hard to start, but still
essential. We don't have to do this all at once. We need to take
it in steps, in small pieces at first, and slowly start to change our
thinking about being uncomfortable, even very uncomfortable
now and again.

5) REFUSING TO DO CONSISTENT SELF-CARE

Self-care provides the foundation we need to tackle this work
of breaking anxiety's hold. It isn't terribly complicated, but it
does run afoul of our fears. In some respects, to deal with anxiety is to have to confront some of the ways we avoid our anxiety
and sabotage our self-care at the same time.

I discuss basic self-care in depth in Chapter 11, but all that
needs to be said here is that we can significantly impair our work
if we won't do those basics. Sleep is fundamental to the extent
that we can improve our sleep. Decent food at regular intervals
gives us the fuel we need to sustain this energy-intensive work.
Some basic physical movement can do wonders for our mental,
physical and emotional health.

Please, don't turn this discussion into another way to abuse yourself mentally and emotionally around all your "failures." That's anxiety talking. See this as a frank discussion of where each of us needs to look clearly at our efforts—or lack thereof—in the direction of self-care.

SO WHAT'S STOPPING YOU IN YOUR WORK?

Everything I've listed in this chapter is completely natural and to be expected as we progress in our work to change anxious thinking to problem thinking, diminish our fear of Flight or Fight, and get much, much better at doing self-care. We're not weak, stupid, brainless or somehow deficient. We're just being human.

Are you stuck right now? That's OK. We can always start up again. Don't really feel like making a move? That's OK too. This isn't about feelings. This is very much about regular, consistent practice, even when we don't really feel like doing it. Convinced that there's something different about your anxiety, or just you as a person? That's all right too. That's just anxiety talking, and you don't have to listen any longer. You have the strength, the capacity and the ability to get free of anxiety.

CHAPTER 17

It Takes Time to Climb Out

Healing is an art. It takes time, it takes practice.
It takes love.
Maza-Dohta

There are few things we'd like to get rid of faster than the habit of anxious thinking. It only makes sense. We are sick of the torment, the flinching back from our lives and the utter drain from our souls in the daily battle with anxiety.

We live in an age when we have come to expect things to move along pretty quickly. We're not accustomed to having to wait for much these days. Microwaves, online shopping, quick weight-

237

loss programs and 1 billion channels of television make it easy to expect to get what we want, NOW.

There is a class of desires, however, that can only come with solid basic thinking skills, good information, regular practice, a learning curve and the bumps that come during that learning curve. For example, want to learn to play the banjo? Scuba dive? Run a marathon? Speak a second language?

You're going to have to practice. And you can't really practice until you have some basic idea of what you're doing in the first place. That practicing is going to take time. You're going to learn some things well, and other things not so well. You'll learn some things wrong, make mistakes, and have to go back and learn them differently.

And no, if banjo is your dream you won't be able to play "Foggy Mountain Breakdown" in 10 days, or even 20. It's going to take some time to master the ancient art of banjo playing. The good news is that it doesn't have to take nearly as much time to break the hold of anxiety as it does to learn to play the banjo. These are skills that in a matter of a few weeks will begin to pay off (with regular practice), and that will grow and spread throughout our thinking.

So—exactly how long does it take to get seriously free of chronic anxiety?

SOLID, BASIC THINKING SKILLS

Thinking is a skill. I know that sounds crazy. Can't everybody just think, the way they just breathe? No. Thinking is actually a fairly complex set of skills. Most of us learn some (but not all) of those skills in two ways: watching/modeling other people, and formal training. This is the first issue in understanding how long our work will take.

Unfortunately most of us learned less-than-adequate thinking skills. We learned instead to make crises out of problems, learned to be afraid of our bodies when Flight or Fight fired up, learned to disregard the basics of self-care, learned to think we should be fiercely self-critical, and learned to run from the thinking that scares us, rather than facing it down and learning to think through it.

....

These skills are doubly important for anxiety fighters who want to hop off the merry-go-round of anxious thinking. Anxiety makes it so easy to just throw up our hands and assume that we're screwed. It takes extra effort to keep our thinking as clear as we can in the face of that tendency.

....

Most of us have to learn at least some of these skills. That learning takes a little time. We're not talking years, but we are talking new (or newish) skills, and skill only comes with practice and time. That learning time isn't a crisis. In fact it's the time we need to build the mental and emotional muscles to deal with anxiety effectively.

There's another issue anxiety brings on: when we're in Flight or Fight it's harder (not impossible, but harder) to keep our thinking clear. That, by itself, is an important skill, and one that only comes with practice and time.

So the speed with which you'll finish this work will depend in part on how effectively you're doing your thinking. This is work anyone can do, but it has to be done. We can't take shortcuts and we can't skimp on doing at least some careful thinking.

GOOD INFORMATION

For the love of all that's holy, there is a lot of bad information and thinking about the nature of anxiety, as well as what we can do about it, floating around out there. Assume that you're screwed—you're just an "anxious person." Do this breathing technique. (While breathwork is very helpful for many of us, it isn't a cure-all.) And a lot more besides.

Lots of anxiety fighters float from theory to theory, teacher to teacher, book to book, technique to technique, flailing for the thing that will give them relief FAST. Sure we do. We're not bad people for doing that, but we're often not doing much to help our efforts to break anxiety's hold, if we're doing this.

We need to ask questions in our search for good information. Is this person someone who has actually dealt with and lived with anxiety? Do they seem to understand what it means to wrestle with anxiety over time? Have they seen good results from the tools and techniques and framework they are advocating?

Finding good information (and vetting/evaluating that information) isn't as easy as looking at someone's credentials or title. Yes, doctors and therapists are in theory supposed to be great resources for getting information about anxiety. Sadly, there are too many doctors and therapists who don't even stop to take a full history of our experience, or listen to our specific experiences. They hear the word "anxiety" and they are already reaching for a prescription pad or recommending desensitization exercises. (Please see Chapter 14 for the discussion about searching for a good therapist as part of this work.)

Part of the problem is they don't really understand anxiety and how it works—conceptually or personally. Medications and desensitization exercises both have a place in this work, even an important place. But they can't by themselves get us free of anxiety. They have to be applied with a strong, solid understanding of how anxiety works and how those tools can best serve that understanding for us.

....

We can't just defer to doctors. We can't just see one

or two therapists and then assume we're screwed

because they couldn't help us effectively.

....

Maybe the best summary of this point is this: are we gathering information, looking at it carefully, looking at who is saying it and asking the questions we need to ask? Or are we assuming that someone who claims to have a way to manage and overcome anxiety must know what they're talking about, and then getting frustrated by our lack of progress? And by the way, I hope you're doing this exact process with this book and with anyone who says they have something useful to say about anxiety. Not all information is equal.

At this point I can imagine hearing some of you say, "Man, this seems like a lot of work. Isn't this tough enough already without having to do this careful research?" Well, in some respects it is a serious hassle. It would be brilliant if we didn't have to work this hard.

On the other hand, it is what it is. We don't always get to pick our battles. But once we've identified that we have a battle to fight, it is up to us to get the best information we can, mostly so we can do our best thinking and work to win that battle. So our speed at overcoming anxiety will depend in part on the quality of information we're using to deal with anxiety.

REGULAR PRACTICE

Practice. I'm reminded of my days as a piano student, back when I thought piano was a grand waste of time. I hated practice. I didn't see the point, I got bored, it was hard.

Except as I got older I realized that to get some things I wanted, I had to get comfortable with the notion of practice. Maybe most kids develop a crappy understanding of practice, but I have come to believe that it isn't so much about practice itself. I think it is more about the fear of failure.

Practice needs to be understood as inexperience working toward experience, and from experience to better and better performance. We're really not clear on the fact that some things we need take time and consistent effort.

Even the word "consistent" is too fraught with the feeling of failure to use with some people. Consistency isn't perfection. Consistency is simply regular practice. Practice is learning, experimenting, trying this and trying that, as well as giving yourself time to get better, slowly, over time.

Practice is not trying it for three days, or two weeks, or for two minutes a day for six months. Practice is not moving from triumph to triumph, consistently improving skill in noticeable ways every time we do practice.

So what is practice? Practice is leaning into the work in a steady, regular way. Practice is a mix of staying clear on our goal, doing the work, staying clear on what we need to practice and expecting every day to be what it is: more effective or less effective, but all of it building upon itself, making us slowly better over time.

Let's get more specific. Practice looks something like this:

1) Having regular sessions reviewing our "what if?" thinking (on paper, on a laptop, on our phone, someplace where we can keep a real, consistent record of our unpacking work), and in that reviewing becoming more and more skillful at seeing our "crises" as problems.

That might mean 10 to 15 minutes, twice a day, three times a day. Maybe before breakfast, after lunch, after dinner. Make a schedule that works for you.

2) Having clear goals and working toward those goals, with the goals centered largely on two things: confronting your old crisis thinking and then replacing it with a problem orientation in the real world. This can't just be done on paper. We have to practice this work in our daily lives, facing down the things that scare us.

If your goal is to get to the corner alone, then do that. While you're doing that, stay clear on how getting to the corner isn't a crisis, whatever your "what if?" fears are shouting at you. Remind yourself that the corner is, for the moment, a problem, and you have ways to manage that problem.

You might do this work three or four or five times in a day. I would really encourage you to come back home and record what happened, how your thinking worked this time, what you can do better, where you're still holding yourself up. Keep a record, please. It will only help.

3) Doing good self-care. How's that sleep thing for you? What are you putting in your face in the way of food? Where are those boundaries you need to draw and maintain?

4) Practicing patience, with yourself more than anyone else. See the work as being practice across time, rather than one heroic effort.

So the speed of our results in breaking anxiety's hold will depend in part on the effort we make to practice.

EXPECT A LEARNING CURVE—INCLUDING THE BUMPS THAT COME WITH ANY LEARNING CURVE

OK. We've tackled good thinking skills, good information and practice. All of that will naturally lead to a learning curve, although maybe it should be called a learning hiking path. You will cover both difficult and easy terrain. Sometimes the path seems unclear or overgrown. Sometimes you hear scary noises in the bushes. And sometimes you get sunburned, and really tired, and grumpy, and you just want a hot shower and a comfortable bed.

Learning is rarely straightforward. We have plateaus, slow places, even back-tracking in a learning curve, a lot like hiking. So what? That's part of learning. It doesn't signal failure and if anything it says that we are learning. And, you guessed it, the speed with which you get clear of crappy, anxious thinking will depend in part on your patience and fortitude in the face of the learning curve/hiking trail.

I have a friend who loves to hike. He hikes pretty much every weekend. He likes to hike at a particular park about an hour from his house, up among the redwood trees. The park he hikes in has a couple of easy trails. It is maybe half a mile or a mile total, mostly flat, very easy to follow. The rest of the park has a variety of trails, some of them miles in length and going over some impressive terrain.

Guess what he notices? Most people who visit this beautiful park stay on the easiest trail, do the shortest walk, and miss the majority of what is available in this location, including the most beautiful views and the most glorious stands of redwood trees. Those people really never see the park—they mostly see the parking lot. The good stuff takes a little work.

We can't get free of anxiety if we won't make the hike. Learning curves are rarely nice, linear, steadily-improving experiences. In the case of rewriting our anxious thinking it will involve experiences like this:

- We face down a fearful thought and it overwhelms us the first two, five, ten, twenty times we try.
- We address one anxious "what if?" thought and four more show up, demanding to be noticed. Normal, not dangerous, but definitely something that can feel overwhelming the first few times it happens. This is a great time to practice letting Flight or Fight just be Flight or Fight and not treat it as if it is actually danger.
- We have a burst of Flight or Fight reactions that "come out of nowhere," what I call aftershocks. (Of course that's not the case. It's always a thought, but it feels like it came out of nowhere.)
- We have a day when we seem to forget everything we've been learning. We're tired, we're distracted, we just feel overwhelmed. This happens with any skill set we seek to learn: playing the piano (or banjo), learning a sport, developing new abilities at work, etc. This just has the added joy of Flight or Fight constantly bumping into us. It's hard, tedious even, but totally within our reach. And of course you haven't lost anything you're learning—you're just in the learning curve.

- We get angry and frustrated! We go to a corner and pout, or break some dishes, or just say screw it, I'll never get this, I suck, etc. Good! Have those days. As a therapist I knew once said, "It's good to have a self-pity party, now and again." Break out the party favors and have that self-pity party. Then take a deep breath and start again.

All of these experiences are natural and normal. They are all part of being in a learning curve. Don't forget how eager anxiety thinking is to get you to give up. Learning a new skill takes time. Learning a small handful of skills, which is what you're doing, will take longer still. It's OK. It's better than OK. These are skills that will be with you the rest of your life.

SO HOW LONG WILL IT TAKE?

I'm sorry (but only a little) to report that there is no clean, simple answer to this, at least chronologically. That's true for any attempt to acquire new skills. I've seen people see substantial relief in just a couple of months. I've also seen people who start, stop, start, stop, start again, taking months and years, but guess what? Most of them make serious progress too. How long it takes depends mostly on the steady, regular work we give this practice.

Hardest of all, I've seen people never really wade in, never really start this work. I'm not putting anyone down. I fought this process tooth and claw. It would be odd if we didn't fight it. It's not comfortable, it rattles the bars of our anxiety cage, and more often than not we don't feel great while we're doing it. But we can't get anywhere if we don't get started and stay with the work, despite how we feel, despite how much we wish it were easier, less scary, etc. It will take the time it takes.

A better question to ask ourselves is, what is getting in our way in this work? Where can we lean in, face down the next obstacle, get better at being uncomfortable so we can get where we want to go?

Another good question to ask is, "How easily do I give up?" Anxiety is so good at teaching us to just surrender, just stop trying, when things get scary and difficult. Even learning to not give up, to not throw in the towel, is a skill, and will take some time to develop.

So are you ready to wade in? There is no time like the present. There's never a perfect time or perfect situation in which to begin this work. Freedom from the burden of chronic, anxious, "what if?" thinking is simply a skill set away.

Erik Kieser

E rik Kieser has had his own experiences with chronic anxiety and panic attacks, which began in early junior high school (early 1974).

After decades of people telling him there was no way to get better, and at the bottom of his fight with anxiety and depression, he began to find a way out. Starting with a small scrap of hope from a visit to a therapist in 1995, Erik has, over the last 22 years, refined his understanding of the nature of anxiety, as well as assembling a toolbox to successfully overcome anxiety. Erik wrote a blog (fearmastery.wordpress.com) chronicling his thinking and explorations in 2010, and from that grew this book.

Erik has a B.A. and M.A. in Speech Communication and has been a business consultant and coach for the last 15 years, working with individuals and teams on a variety of critical thinking and communication skills (lucidthinking.com). Born and raised in Las Vegas, Nevada, Erik currently lives in Los Angeles, California.

Bibliography/Further Reading

Beattie, Melody. *Codependent No More.* **Hazelden, 1992.**
Ms. Beattie is one of the pioneers in understanding and dealing with the terrible nature of codependency (one of the ways, I would argue, we respond to anxious thinking), and this book is one of the best sources I've found for understanding and developing healthy personal boundaries.

Carson, Richard & Bailey, Joseph. *Slowing Down to the Speed of Life.* **Harper San Francisco, 1997.**
This isn't so much a book about anxiety as it is a guide to simply slowing down and being more in the present moment. There is a great deal of material these days around mindfulness and present-moment thinking, but in my opinion this is the gold standard.

Duhigg, Charles. *The Power of Habit.* **The Random House Group, Limited, 2012.**
While many people these days are writing about the burgeoning science of habits, Mr. Duhigg does a brilliant job of explaining both how habits are shaped and what we can do to alter them.

Elliott, Charles H. PhD & Smith, Laura L., PhD. *Overcoming Anxiety for Dummies.* **Wiley Publishing, 2002.**
This is a wonderful collection of tactics and strategies for dealing with anxious thinking, as well as managing Flight or Fight.

Ellis, Albert, PhD. *Feeling Better, Getting Better, Staying Better.* **Impact, 2002.**
Ellis, Albert, PhD. *A New Guide to Rational Living.* **Wilshire Book Company, 1975.**
Dr. Ellis is one of the giants of Cognitive-Behavior Therapy, and these two books are only a strong sample of the many he's written on this subject. While both books were fundamental to my writing, I in particular recommend *Feeling Better, Getting Better, Staying Better* as an ongoing resource for those of us who learn to think anxiously.

Jeffers, Susan, PhD. *Feel the Fear and Do It Anyway.* **Fawcett Books, 1987.**
Jeffers, Susan, PhD. *Embracing Uncertainty.* **St. Martin's Griffin, 2003.**
Dr. Jeffers is truly one of the pioneers of facing down anxiety, and *Feel the Fear* is a watershed book that has some excellent advice on practical ways to think about and actively face into anxious thinking. *Embracing Uncertainty* contains what I might call more advanced work for us anxiety fighters, specifically addressing the "big" questions about death, illness, etc.—i.e., the problems that we can't do anything about, but which we can reframe and learn to not treat as crises.

Rubin, Theodore Isaac, M.D. *Compassion & Self-Hate, an Alternative to Despair.* **Touchstone, 1975.**
This is possibly the most important book I've ever read with regard to understanding how anxiety takes hold and grows

through our thinking. While Dr. Rubin identifies anxiety as self-hate in his book it is my argument that self-hate springs from anxious thinking, and that the two terms, to a significant degree, are interchangeable. The second half of the book, in which he discusses the nature of and the need for self-compassion, should be mandatory reading in our schools.

Seagrave, Ann & Covington, Faison. *Free From Fears*. Pocket Books, 1989.
This is the book that started my journey out of anxious thinking. It is part of a mixed-media program offered through the CHAANGE Program, currently run by Dr. John Pullen. (You'll find a website link in the Resources Appendix of this book.) These two women, together with their therapist, created a program for addressing anxiety based on their experience, which is what grew into CHAANGE. The book has some very practical advice for dealing with Flight or Fight reactions and getting out of the immediate crisis thinking that Flight or Fight can drive so fiercely.

Seligman, Martin E., PhD. *Learned Optimism*. Vintage Books, 2006.
Seligman, Martin E., PhD. *Authentic Happiness*. Free Press, 2002.
Dr. Seligman and his fellow researchers have done ground-breaking work developing the notion of "learned helplessness," which is instrumental in understanding how anxiety takes hold of our thinking and drives the habit of retreating from our fears. He has a great deal more to say to anxiety fighters in regard to healthy thinking, and I highly recommend both of these books!

Sapolsky, Robert M. *Why Zebras Don't Get Ulcers.* **Henry Holt & Company, 2004.**
This is both a highly informative and entertaining look at the nature of Flight or Fight and how it drives our behavior.

Sarno, John E., PhD. *The Mindbody Prescription.* **Warner Books, 1998.**
Another groundbreaking book (and, oddly, still controversial in some circles) that is about the way thinking can drive reactions in the human body, including lots of symptoms that mimic serious health problems. This is great stuff for getting under our fears of Flight or Fight reactions.

Weil, Andrew, M.D. *Spontaneous Happiness.* **Little, Brown & Company, 2011.**
Perhaps the best summary of this beautifully written and lucid book is that it is a discussion of what mental and emotional health looks like, and practices that can take us there.

Resources

PHONE NUMBERS

911 — If it's an emergency in which you or someone you know is in crisis, you should call 911 or go to a hospital emergency room.

1-800-273-8255 — The National Suicide Prevention Lifeline provides 24/7, free and confidential support for people in distress, and prevention and crisis resources for you or your loved ones.

1-800-950-6264 — The National Alliance on Mental Illness Helpline is open 10 a.m. to 6 p.m. (Eastern time) Monday through Friday. You can also text "NAMI" to 741741 for help.

Add contact information for your local resources.

Name: _____
Number: _____

Name: _____
Number: _____

Name: _____
Number: _____

Add contact information for friends you can call for help.

Name: _____
Number: _____

Name: _____
Number: _____

Name: _____
Number: _____

Name: _____
Number: _____

USEFUL WEBSITES

www.NAMI.org — The National Alliance on Mental Illness has an excellent list of online resources as well as many local chapters with lists of local resources.

www.SuicidePreventionLifeline.org — The National Suicide Prevention Lifeline has additional information and resources at its website.

www.SAMHSA.gov— The Substance Abuse and Mental Health Services Administration has some useful resource lists.

My3App.org — This organization offers a free app for IOS and Android that provides quick access to three friends to support you if you are in crisis.

THERAPIST SEARCH WEBSITES

www.PsychologyToday.com
Psychology Today has a service to help you search for mental health professionals.

www.GoodTherapy.org
Another service for searching for mental health professionals.

FindTreatment.SAMHSA.gov
SAMHSA has a service for finding low-cost/sliding-scale mental health services. Phone 800-662-4357.

Made in the USA
Middletown, DE
30 June 2018